THE
NEW
REASON
TO
WORK

THE NEW REASON TO WORK

How to Build a Career
That Will Change the World

ROSHAN PAUL & ILAINA RABBAT

LIONCREST
PUBLISHING

THE NEW REASON TO WORK
How to Build a Career That Will Change the World

ISBN   978-1-5445-2516-7   *Hardcover*
      978-1-5445-2517-4   *Paperback*
      978-1-5445-2518-1   *Ebook*

CONTENTS

For those with the courage to reimagine the meaning of work
and the determination to make a career
out of changing the world.

In other words, this is for you.

Dear Ruchika,

    I hope you enjoy another approach to purpose. I look forward to reading yours as well!

        Roshan

I hope you enjoy another

PART I

INTRODUCTION

1

THE NEW REASON TO WORK

For both of us, our preconceived notions of the person we'd be meeting, on that life-altering day in August 2010, were wrong. But we were both wrong in the exact same way.

"She looks a lot younger than I imagined," I, Roshan, thought, standing up to welcome Ilaina to my office. Though I knew she'd been my colleague for several years, seeing this slim young woman, no taller than five feet, with long brown hair and braces on her teeth, I couldn't help but think that she was still in her late teens. Only once we'd begun talking did I start to realize that her forthright voice and confident eyes indicated that she was no teenager, but someone with more than a decade of experience in stepping up to change the world.

We met on a typically muggy summer afternoon in Washington, DC, the capital city of the country with the largest number of impact-first jobs in the world. Less than two years after Barack Obama took office, the Washington area still basked in the euphoria and optimism from the election of a young, black president. The financial crash of 2008 seemed to be slowly ebbing, but the Tea Party revolt that would reshape America was gathering steam, and the Arab Spring was a few short months away. At the time, I was leading a project at Ashoka, the global nonprofit organization best known for its work in developing the field of social entrepreneurship, to support social entrepreneurs in conflict zones. I hadn't always thought I'd be doing this, though.

As a college student in the United States at the turn of the century, I assumed I would have a career in management consulting or investment banking, which is what most of my peers, other foreign students in America, were aiming for.

But on a beautiful Tuesday in September, at the start of my senior year of college, I finished my early morning French class and walked over to the cafeteria for a cup of coffee. I noticed a group of people clustered around a TV screen. As I reached them, I saw the second plane hit the second of the twin towers of the World Trade Center in New York City. Along with my classmates, I watched in horror as people jumped out of those gigantic buildings. I watched them fall, and then I saw the second tower collapse. Later that evening, the university president—a middle-aged, religious white man running a very conservative and very Christian school—gathered the whole student body together and said that if any foreign students or minority Americans were targeted in the weeks and months to come, the university would put all its resources toward protecting those students. Even now, I remember 9/11 like it was yesterday. I vividly remember the feeling that the horror of the morning, and the unlikely but courageous leadership shown that evening, had just framed the defining day of my adult life.

In the months following that tragedy, with racial attacks on people with brown skin on the rise across the United States and rising violence between Hindus and Muslims in my native country of India, the two nations I knew best seemed to be on fire. As I trudged from one interview to another, I couldn't help thinking, "What would be the point of working in management consulting, helping an oil company save money, or an insurance company streamline processes?" Unable to answer that question satisfactorily, I retreated from my job interviews with such firms.

One of those firms was the global consulting giant McKinsey & Company. When I let them know that I was no longer interested in working with them, they were surprised. Who backs away from McKinsey? *And*, in a recession year? Clearly intrigued, they invited me in to speak with a Partner at the firm. Nervously fiddling with the buttons of my ill-fitting suit as I sat outside the Partner's office, I expected either a hard sell on the money I would make and prestige I would gain there, or dismissive scorn at the prospect of working in social impact instead. But when he heard me out, to my astonishment, the

Partner nodded and said, "Prior to joining McKinsey, I spent ten years as a musician traveling with a band. I learned so much and it made me a better consultant. If you really want to do this, then go for it! I wish you luck."

I left his office, still uncertain about whether I would find a job, but more confident that I was right to follow my intuition. I didn't yet know that we only connect the dots of our life choices in hindsight. Upon graduating, I returned to India where I shocked my friends and family by accepting a job in social entrepreneurship at a salary of $200 a month. Over the next decade, while working to serve hundreds of social entrepreneurs all around the world, I slowly began to realize the fulfillment that comes from making an impact with one's career.

Eventually, many of the people who initially thought me crazy for turning my back on management consulting in favor of a low-paying nonprofit job in India, came to see me holding a relatively senior role in a highly regarded global nonprofit organization, with frequent international travel and invitations to lecture at famous universities. They began asking for advice on how they, too, could switch careers, eager to make a difference in the world while building a thriving career.

* * *

"He's not as old as I was expecting," I, Ilaina thought, knocking on the open door to Roshan's office on the twentieth floor of Ashoka's corporate office building. His short and formal way of responding to emails and his picture on the organization website, wearing serious-looking glasses, made him seem in his fifties, but when I saw him, he had the youthful ease of movement you might more associate with a sportsman, and the fresh smile of someone with charm and energy.

As someone who had been interested in peacebuilding for over a decade and was working in the same sprawling global organization, I wanted to learn more about the project Roshan was leading to help social entrepreneurs in societies torn apart by conflict. My connection to peacebuilding started even before I was born. My parents were forced to flee their native Argentina, their lives in danger after Jorge Rafael Videla's military coup kicked off one of the darkest times in Argentine history.

Growing up in Venezuela and Argentina with talk of freedom, equality, and human rights as much a part of everyday family dinners as *arepas* and *milanesas,* I inculcated those ideals and made them my life's mission, even without consciously realizing it at the time. By elementary school, I was already organizing campaigns to take care of the environment and assist people with basic needs. In high school, I began to collaborate with a local nongovernmental organization (NGO), the Argentinian Youth Organization for the United Nations, to prepare active citizens who would proactively solve global problems. Even then, I dreamed of working with the United Nations or an international NGO, but I had no idea how to get there.

In university, I decided to do my international relations undergraduate thesis on the role of international NGOs in Haiti, with the intention to use it as an excuse to go to Haiti and find a job. I had been intrigued by Haiti ever since I read *The Kingdom of This World* by Alejo Carpentier, in which he narrates how Haiti became the second independent country in the Americas after the first successful slave revolt in history. I interviewed everyone I could find in Argentina who had worked in Haiti, but my dream was traveling to Haiti to do field research. I decided I would go, even though the Argentinian Embassy in Haiti told me they would not let me in since kidnappings of businessmen, students, aid workers, and foreigners were commonplace. They said—with reason, although it made me very upset then— that they wouldn't take responsibility for an *irresponsible student*. Against all odds, a few months later, I landed in Port-au-Prince, invited by a Dominican Republic organization and traveling in armored cars, to present my thesis at a conference in Haiti. After many years of unrest, Haiti had made important progress toward restoring democratic rule, and there was an air of optimism.

However, everything had changed by the time I returned to Haiti after the 2010 earthquake, volunteering with Techo, an organization that helped build temporary housing for the more than 1.5 million newly internally displaced people. I still remember seeing the Presidential Palace in pieces and viewing, from a hill at Jacmel, the endless rows of improvised plastic refugee tents, and asking myself how this could have happened. It took me many years to recover from what I saw and experienced in Haiti, but it only took me days to understand that I needed to do something else to help prevent things like that from continuing to happen. It was no longer about working in an international NGO (as I was already doing); it was about rethinking how we look at solving global problems together.

Just a few weeks after that visit to Haiti, on that fateful August day in 2010, I knocked on the office door of a colleague who I'd assumed would be at least a couple of decades older than me.

THE MEANING OF WORK IS CHANGING

As we look back on our first meeting, where we passionately discussed how changemakers could play a key role in post-conflict societies, we are aware that although we each started our career in social impact at a young age, that's not how most people come to this type of career. There are huge numbers of people who have no idea that such a career even exists. This is not what we're raised to think of as work. The *Cambridge Dictionary* defines work as an "activity, such as a job, that a person uses physical or mental effort to do, usually for money." However, the *reason* we go to work has evolved across generations. For our earliest ancestors, work was about securing the most basic human needs: food, childcare, and shelter. Depending on your sex or your age, you might be caring for the youngest in the tribe or you might be going hunting. Later, as humans settled in cities and the Industrial Revolution changed the economy, work not only allowed you to make a living, but also became a source of identity and self-worth by conferring status, power, and recognition—especially if you weren't born with those privileges. People grew conscious of things such as titles and salaries and management levels as means by which others would evaluate them.

But relax! We'll spare you an exhaustive review of the evolution of work in human society. Yet, this brief background is important, because there's been a gradual shift in recent years. A growing number of people from all backgrounds and ages are starting to challenge the traditional reasons we go to work. Like them, we don't believe that work is or should be transactional anymore (i.e., the lending of hours, expertise, and effort in return for money, power, and status.) We're increasingly aware of a new variable in the equation: *impact.*

Impact is the value your job creates in the world beyond the immediate benefits to you or your employers. It is what you leave behind when you're gone. It is the extent to which society is better off because you were in it. We believe that the future of work is one in which your job description includes not only your title, responsibilities, and salary, but also a convincing case for the impact your work will create.

WHAT IS IMPACT WORK?

Throughout this book, we define impact work or impact-first jobs as those where you use the *majority* of your time and effort with the primary intention to improve the human and/or planetary condition, instead of just your own or your organization's bottom line. It's where social impact is not a possible side-benefit, but, in fact, the core purpose of the job, where your day is organized around moving toward impact. The most critical thing to note at this stage is that all this can be true *regardless* of what sector or type of job you hold.

For example, it is easy to understand how someone working for a nonprofit, say managing a health program in a slum in Nairobi, is engaged in social impact work. But it might be less clear with other jobs.

Let's imagine a company selling soap to low-income people in that slum in Nairobi. The owner of the company may not be selling soap for any other reason than there's a market for it—all humans need soap. However, perhaps that same owner seeks to improve hygiene in that population to help reduce disease and illness, and thus produces more affordable soap. The second scenario is impact work, because the goals are different. Goals and intentions matter because they determine how you create your product and how you make decisions about the business. Impact work is about the social problem that a product or service seeks to solve. It is about meeting a societal need, not exploiting a market opportunity. In the first scenario, the owner's intention is to meet needs such as making money, growing a company, and so on; in the second, the owner wants to increase overall health in the slum, and selling soap is simply one way to do that.

Now let's consider an employee of the soap company—we'll call him Omar. If the company is not impact-driven (i.e., it just wants to make a profit selling soap) does it follow that Omar will never be able to have an impact at work? Not necessarily! Let's say that Omar is the salesman who goes door-to-door selling soap. He can still decide to make his job impact-driven by *"using the majority of his time and effort to improve the human condition."* Seeing that more soap usage leads to fewer illnesses (and thus fewer days of missed work or school), he spends time with each prospective customer explaining how to use the soap properly. While this might decrease his productivity, it might also increase the value of each sale, since every buyer will now understand the lifetime importance of using soap and keep buying soap from Omar and his company. Even if Omar's boss only cares about the bottom line, Omar can see the possibility of a larger purpose for his daily work. And thus, Omar's job is impact-first, and he is likely to be more fulfilled than his boss.

What about professions such as teaching, nursing, and medicine? We might assume they have social impact embedded in them, simply by virtue of the fact that practitioners of these professions help other people every day. But if we look at the definition of impact or impact-first jobs, we see that not all teachers or doctors qualify. Unless the *intent* of their work goes beyond themselves or the immediate person they are helping or the institution they work for, we wouldn't consider it impact-first. In other words, it is not about improving a single student's skills or the school's rank in mathematics, but about thinking bigger than that (i.e., using the majority of their time and effort with the primary intention to improve the human and/or planetary condition).

One example of someone who did so is the late Gloria de Souza, a primary school teacher in Mumbai, India. Dreaming of changing the education system in India, she started Parisar Asha, an organization now known for having developed the curriculum called Environmental Studies (EVS). At its time in the 1980s, EVS was a pioneering approach to education that challenged students to think and to solve problems together, while focusing on attitudes and values. De Souza's work went beyond just teaching her students; it was about improving education for all, and it became part of the national curriculum in India. That is how Roshan, who grew up in Bengaluru, quite far from Mumbai, was able to study EVS. It was his favorite subject as a kid.

There can be any number of ways of making an impact with your work. This book is based on the principle that impact work is here to stay because more and more people are demanding impact as a prerequisite of their job. When you extend that trend further, a new world starts to come into view, one in which the reason to work itself has changed.

THE RISING DEMAND FOR IMPACT WORK

In the next chapter, we will describe how the evolution of impact-first work has led to a vast array of career opportunities. Part of the reason for this dramatic increase in opportunities is a rising demand for them. The reason we *want* to work is changing.

Over the past hundred years—at least, if not longer—each generation's baseline standard of living has gotten better than their predecessors'. Some of the physical comforts enjoyed by the poor today would have been considered luxurious by living standards one hundred years ago. Technological progress has been the biggest reason for this—it is ever-cheaper to be more comfortable (at least physically). Extending this trend into the decades to come and considering the possibilities created by automation and 3D printing, it's easy to envision a world where it will become less and less important to work for money. And once humans take care of their own basic needs, they move toward higher-order needs, such as achieving their potential and finding meaning in their lives.

We often hear the trite exhortations: *find your purpose* or *follow your passion!* The problem is that these are often framed in the context of one's self. We ask: what is *my* purpose? That gets trite because it is easy for your sense of purpose to remain between your ears or inside your heart, and never change anything. What does change things, and what *never* gets stale, is making a difference in the lives of others. The emotional and psychological satisfaction from doing so far exceeds that coming from simply accumulating more wealth. From inner purpose comes outward impact. Ancient religions have always known this, and modern psychology confirms it. We benefit by helping everyone do so.

Indeed, there is a gradual but burgeoning realization that working toward impact provides many more benefits than not doing so. We can now measure and demonstrate that people who work toward impact have a greater likelihood of enjoying higher job satisfaction, life satisfaction, and even better physical and mental health![1]

For instance, the Happiness Research Institute found that a sense of purpose is not only *the biggest predictor* of job satisfaction, but that it ranks twice as high as the next thing on the list (which, by the way, is having a good manager).[2] Even in the private sector, the best managers know that they need to manage their teams more toward attaining a greater purpose than simply making money. That study also found that purpose did not mean something easy, but rather the opposite—that striving toward a challenging goal you care about is most strongly correlated to your happiness.

From all this, a trend is emerging: the quest for building a career, and a life, of impact. More and more people, especially those under thirty-five today, their faith in big institutions shattered by the financial crisis of 2008 and movements ranging from Occupy Wall Street to #metoo to Black Lives Matter, are willing to earn less if they can do work that makes a difference. They're willing to trade money for meaning, profits for purpose.

---

1   Amy Wrzesniewski, Clark McCauley, Paul Rozin, and Barry Schwartz, "Jobs, Careers, and Callings: People's Relations to Their Work," *Journal of Research in Personality* 31, no. 1 (March 1997): 21–33, http://dx.doi.org/10.1006/jrpe.1997.2162; Christopher Peterson, Nansook Park, Nicholas Hall, and Martin E. P. Seligman, "Zest and Work," Journal of Organizational Behavior 30, no. 2 (February 2009): 161–172, http://dx.doi.org/10.1002/job.584.

2   *Happiness Research Institute, Job Satisfaction Index 2015: What Drives Job Satisfaction?*, 2015, https://www.happinessresearchinstitute.com/publications.

Consider the organization Escape the City, which helps people find more fulfilling careers. They began in London in 2010 with fifty members. Today, they have grown to *500,000 people* from more than one hundred countries.[3] Some of them have come to study with us. There is a hunger, everywhere, for careers of meaning.

AMANI INSTITUTE–OR WHY IT'S US WRITING THIS BOOK

If the primary reason we work changes, how we prepare for work should also change.

Our first conversation on that summer day in 2010—about changemakers in conflict-ridden countries—led to a deeper discussion about the role changemakers play everywhere, and how our current higher education systems were not preparing them for careers in the growing world of social impact. As summer turned into fall, our conversations got deeper. We began to envision a new organization, one that would answer the question: what is the right education for social impact careers?

Two years later, in July 2012, we were landing at Jomo Kenyatta International Airport, craning our necks to see giraffes from the airplane window. Nairobi National Park is the world's only wildlife sanctuary inside a capital city, and it is right next to the

---

3   "Find Work that Matters to You and the World," Escape the City Ltd., accessed July 13, 2021, https://www.escapethecity.org/about?v=story.

international airport. While the park is home to rhino, zebra, lions, and many other species, giraffes are, of course, the easiest to see from an airplane.

After nearly two years of research about the future of higher education and the needs of employers in the years to come, we decided to quit our jobs at Ashoka to develop a new organization: Amani Institute. We gave ourselves one year to see if we could make it happen. In the year that followed, many people wondered aloud why we would consider leaving jobs we enjoyed at a globally reputed organization to start something new. After all, as many people hinted to Roshan, who in their right mind leaves a stable job in America to start a nonprofit in Africa? Or as others queried Ilaina, why drop the dream of working in an international NGO to build a startup?

Indeed, it may have seemed most logical to launch Amani Institute in the United States. We both lived there at the time, and it is the likeliest place where we may have received funding and other support. Yet that didn't sit right with us. Having grown up in emerging markets, we knew that they represented the frontiers of social change. But most world-class educational institutions are in high-income societies. We wanted to flip that dynamic by intentionally locating ourselves where the world is changing most rapidly, where you can see the future.

We chose Nairobi because it is one of the most innovative emerging market cities on the planet. It was a huge gamble, because we were arriving in Nairobi without a team, customers, funding, or even a website.

The gamble paid off. We set out to create an institution that would offer specialized training for professionals who wish to solve the world's most challenging problems. We wanted to build for others a career path around the idea that making a difference can be a *profession*, not a hobby, nor a passion project, nor a pursuit for those without anything better to do. We would develop a practical education for a global audience, located firmly in the new centers of innovation in the world: Nairobi, São Paulo, and Bangalore. Kenya, Brazil, and India. From modest little offices in these three vibrant cities, we have supported the leadership and professional growth of changemakers around the world, having trained, as of 2020, more than 540 "Amani Fellows" through our award-winning Certificate in Social Innovation Management, more than twenty-five hundred young leaders through the Young African Leadership Initiative, and senior managers from more than seventy businesses in East Africa and India. In addition, we've strengthened the internal capacity of more than one hundred organizations across five continents through a range of different talent development projects. We've also brought many thousands of people together in more than a dozen countries to attend unique events related to the future of work, twenty-first century careers, network building, and social innovation. Over the span of all this work, Amani Institute had, almost without our noticing it, become a notable contributor to the global conversation about the future of work. Perhaps most importantly, it was one of the few such contributors rooted in the Global South. You will learn more about our work in the following chapters, largely through the stories of ordinary individuals who, like us, set out to use their careers to make a difference in the world. And while we initially set out to train people to work in the social sector, over the years we came to understand that we have been preparing them for the future of work itself, one in which increasing numbers of jobs will be impact-first.

THIS BOOK IS FOR YOU

This book is about how what we've learned throughout our careers, over nearly two decades each, points to that emerging future. We share the insights and the lessons that helped us unlock the impact careers of thousands of people literally all over the world. If you are about to graduate or are a recent graduate with a bachelor's or master's degree and you want to build a social impact career from the get-go, this book is for you. When we started Amani Institute, it was you we wanted to serve.

As we got down to work in Nairobi and beyond, we discovered another exciting audience: brave people willing to change their careers to build a legacy they can be proud of. If you are currently in a job or career that you find lacks a larger meaning and you want to reinvent yourself to make a difference to the lives of others, this book is for you too.

Finally, let's say you are already working toward social impact. Are you feeling stuck, disillusioned, or unfulfilled by your work? If so, you will find the perspectives and practices outlined in this book extremely valuable toward making a shift toward a more satisfying impact-first career.

We are not academics or researchers. Although we've both studied at leading universities in the United States, we grew up in very different parts of the Global South and have spent the majority of our working lives in Latin America, East Africa, and South Asia. Our perspective is formed by all these experiences. It is truly global. Throughout the book, we will adopt the lens of the practitioner grappling with multiple perspectives and sometimes contradictory data, striving to take the best—but never perfect or ideal—course of action in complicated settings. This book is about making change in the messy, real world.

AN OVERVIEW

We begin by sharing a layperson's history of the field you want to join and casting a bird's-eye view over what opportunities are available for you today, exploring why there has never been a better time to consider careers that make a difference, as well as how to choose among the wide range of available options.

Armed with an understanding of the history and landscape of impact-first careers, and based on our combined forty years of experience of working toward social impact and helping thousands of others build their own impact-first careers, we have identified six keys that are essential to unlock your dream career in social impact, laid out in the following six chapters.

The core premise of Chapter 3 is that, since the foundations of work are changing, a new way of education is needed for this new world of work. We show you how to pursue the kind of education that sets you up to thrive in this world. In Chapter 4, we challenge the belief that our professional and personal lives are separate. Rather than "work-life balance," a far better way is to align who we are with what we do. Chapter 5 demonstrates the importance of becoming a social innovator, your direct passport to making an impact *independent* of your job, and simple and effective ways in which everyone can build the skill of social innovation.

Chapter 6 acknowledges that any impact work is collective. This chapter helps you weave a meaningful global network that will spur you on to greater heights. Chapter 7 is about how to own and tell your story in the service of your impact career—and why that only gets more important all the time. Once you have unlocked the door to a career of impact, Chapter 8, our sixth and final key, is about keeping that door open, to both prepare for and sustain yourself over a career-long marathon instead of a quick sprint.

This book is also full of stories that illustrate these six keys, both our own personal stories as well as the stories of many inspiring-but-ordinary individuals also leading impact-first careers. In addition, most of the chapters also have exercises, woven into the narrative itself, that will help you practice that chapter's content to advance your own impact-first career. We end each chapter with some questions for reflection and some initial steps you can take to put these ideas into practice.

But first, you will meet two other people who will accompany you on your journey through this book. Kim and Farah are *fictional characters*, composites from the thousands of aspiring changemakers we have encountered in our work. They appear as your guides, and hopefully they will ask us the types of questions that you would.

Let's go meet them and dive in!

2

THE EVOLUTION OF IMPACT WORK

MEETING KIM AND FARAH

We, Ilaina and Roshan, were in a good mood at the end of the event. At Amani Institute, we frequently host evening events to raise awareness about impact-first careers, and how the range of options for such careers are ever-expanding. This particular event had been excellent, complete with a highly engaged audience participating with gusto and asking great questions. We stayed behind after the event finished, taking final questions one-on-one. When the last person was done, we zipped up our bags and headed to the door, still feeling energized by how the evening had gone. We noticed two of the attendees talking animatedly outside. They turned toward us as we exited the building.

"Thanks for a great event," the woman said. She was tall with long, straight brown hair, and Arab or possibly Latin American features. She extended her hand with a warm smile. "I'm Farah, and I really enjoyed the conversations. As you can see, we're still going, even out here," she said, nodding at her companion.

"Hey, that was great," he chimed in, seemingly bursting with energy. He was shorter than her, with curly blond hair and a clipped Anglo-Saxon accent. "We're still debating some of the things you both said."

We immediately warmed to them—not just because of their positive energy toward us, but because, like us, they seemed to belong to that group of people who identify as citizens of the world instead of a single nationality, people who instinctively see the world as one interconnected whole, filled with human beings sharing similar dreams and fears.

The young man added, "We were just about to grab a bite to eat. Would you like to join us? I'm Kim, by the way."

We looked at each other. Our plan for the evening was also to go eat dinner, so why not join them? We walked over to a nearby cafe and dropped into an easy conversation.

"I came to your event because I am thinking of quitting my job," Farah said. "I've been working in both small and large companies as a designer for about ten years. I love the actual design work, but I'm tired of doing it to sell products that I no longer believe in or for organizations that see their employees as just cogs in a wheel. The final straw was when one of my female teammates was offered a directorship role but at a 20 percent lower salary than her male co-director. This triggered a lot of questions about what fairness and justice at work mean to me, the deeper aims behind my work, and the role of women in the workplace. I want to continue being a designer, but I want to use my skills for things that matter."

After thanking Farah for sharing her story and lauding her bravery to be willing to reconsider her career choices, we turned to Kim.

"I've just graduated from university, and I've been trying to figure out the range of job options available. I studied economics and drove my professors crazy with questions that challenged the dominant economic model, so much that I would earn eye-rolls from my own classmates," Kim said, then paused with a wry grin before adding, "although sometimes also to some applause. While researching alternative economic models, I became interested in climate change. I see a fundamental disconnect between capitalism and the planet's ability to cope. We need more people working on better ways to organize economic output. In the event, you mentioned that the number of impact-first jobs has been increasing throughout history and will eventually become the norm. But you didn't explain how that happened and what jobs exactly are out there for people like me. I'd like to learn more about that."

"Sure! Let me first say that we highly value the people who dare to challenge the status quo. It will not always be an easy path, but it can be very rewarding," Ilaina said. She picked up a napkin and began to draw on it. "What we meant is that the impact-first sector grew from being a small sector with a handful of job opportunities to becoming a vast array of organizations and jobs across the whole economy. We rarely talk about just the social sector anymore. You also find impact-first jobs in both the public and private sectors because, thanks to a few major turning points in the evolution of the social impact sector, new ways of looking at work and organizing our economy are emerging."

The waitress came up with our drinks and took our dinner orders and menus. Kim took a big gulp of his drink and then, leaning forward with hands crossed and elbows on the table, said, "Tell me more about those turning points and the creation of impact-first jobs. What was the original social sector you mentioned? Why and how is it expanding and changing? I'm still in student mode," he said with a laugh. "Tell me the history!"

THE LANDSCAPE OF IMPACT WORK IN EIGHT TURNING POINTS

Roshan laughed too. "Maybe we'll get into professor mode then!" he said. "I can try and summarize the history as we see it, focusing on more recent and global trends. But I will certainly leave out important historical events and of course can't cover what the social sector is like in any single country, so forgive me in advance for that. But this will serve as a working knowledge of the field of social impact. Does that work for you?"

Kim and Farah nodded.

"All right," said Roshan, mentally organizing his thoughts. "Let's walk through the evolution of the modern, global, social sector, framed around key turning points."

"And while Roshan explains the turning points, I will point out what new jobs each turning point brought," Ilaina added.

THE EVOLUTION OF IMPACT WORK

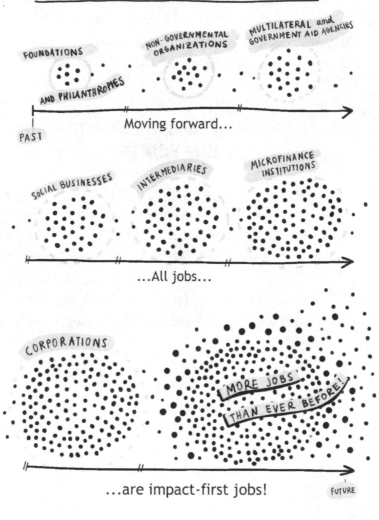

FOUNDATIONS
AND PHILANTHROPES

NON-GOVERNMENTAL ORGANIZATIONS

MULTILATERAL and GOVERNMENT AID AGENCIES

PAST

Moving forward...

SOCIAL BUSINESSES

INTERMEDIARIES

MICROFINANCE INSTITUTIONS

...All jobs...

CORPORATIONS

MORE JOBS THAN EVER BEFORE!

...are impact-first jobs!

FUTURE

Roshan began, "The first turning point was probably in the 1890s, with **the rise of philanthropy**. When American industrialist Andrew Carnegie famously pronounced that, 'The man who dies rich, dies disgraced,' he kicked off the modern philanthropy movement that soon included people like John D. Rockefeller, Henry Ford, and others. None of these wealthy businessmen were saints, to put it mildly, and they may well have had ulterior motives for their actions. That said, by giving away large chunks of their fortunes, they implicitly acknowledged that neither government nor business could solve for everything humans need, and another group of institutions was needed to help society address shared problems. This was a new notion at the time. And the money they put behind it led to the first spurt of new organizations specifically set up to address social issues.

"The second turning point was **the rise of international nongovernmental organizations, or NGOs**. There have always been volunteers and do-gooders looking out for the less privileged. And the first NGOs came into being well before the rise of philanthropy. But it was not until the first half of the twentieth century that they really came into prominence, thanks to the havoc wreaked by the two world wars. Perhaps no organization symbolizes the NGO more than the International Committee for the Red Cross. Although it was founded in the 1860s, it jumped into the limelight during World War I. Its famous "doctrine of neutrality"—treating all victims of war equally, regardless of which side they represented—became the centerpiece of humanitarian action and is still seen as dogma by many organizations even today. It has also won three Nobel Peace Prizes—not bad for a single organization!

"And yet, it is by no means the only one! Here are the names and founding dates of some of the world's largest NGOs today: Save the Children (1919), International Rescue Committee (1933), Oxfam (1942), CARE (1945), World Vision (1950), World Wildlife Fund (1961), and Amnesty International (1961).

"These organizations are important because they are still the biggest ones in the impact-first sector. They have been around for several decades and work in hundreds of countries. They have probably outlasted 99 percent of private companies that were founded after them, so let nobody tell you that only businesses can scale! More importantly, they have collectively saved and improved hundreds of millions of lives."

Then Ilaina jumped in. "These first two turning points launched the first set of traditional impact-first jobs. They are still the nucleus of impact-first work, because you are almost guaranteed to have impact through them—the definition of impact being where the majority of your time is spent trying to improve the human and/or planetary condition. This is where the industry of impact-first careers got started. Today, there are jobs in foundations or philanthropies and in a variety of NGOs: humanitarian NGOs, human rights NGOs, development NGOs, and local NGOs or community-based organizations. Let's take them one by one."

"Yes please, because they look all the same to me!" Farah said.

Nodding in understanding, Ilaina continued, *"Foundations and philanthropies* use private capital and/or crowdsourced donations to provide funding to social impact organizations working directly with needy populations, usually in the form of grants (donations that do not have to be repaid). They can be either purely charitable or very strategic in their giving. A large amount of philanthropic funding is also religiously motivated—some goes toward social impact, some of it doesn't. Examples of large and well-known foundations around the world include: Bill & Melinda Gates Foundation, The Rockefeller Foundation, Ford Foundation, Children's Investment Fund Foundation, and Stichting DOEN.

"Now let's move on to the different types of NGOs. *Humanitarian NGOs* respond to emergency situations, usually in times of natural disasters or conflicts, providing short-term material and logistical aid, with the focus on saving lives and reducing suffering. Examples of renowned humanitarian NGOs include the various Red Cross and Red Crescent organizations, International Rescue Committee, Doctors Without Borders/Medecins Sans Frontieres, Save the Children, Catholic Relief Services, and the Norwegian Refugee Council.

"By contrast, *Human Rights NGOs* focus on protecting the rights of disadvantaged populations, reducing conflict, and promoting justice. Examples are Amnesty International, Human Rights Watch, Committee to Protect Journalists, and the Centro Latinoamericano de Derechos Humanos (CLADH).

"On the other hand, *Development NGOs* focus on long-term economic and social progress, usually in lower- and middle-income countries. They are probably the second largest category of impact organizations. Most countries have several well-known development NGOs at national scale. Some famous global ones include Habitat for Humanity, World Wildlife Fund, Aga Khan Development Network, Teach for All, Building Resources Across Communities (BRAC), Plan International, and Un Techo Para Mi País (TECHO). Some of these also provide the same services as humanitarian NGOs.

"Lastly, *Local NGOs and Community-Based Organizations* focus on economic and social development in a specific, and often relatively small, geographic area—either individual communities, rural districts, or in one city. They are the largest category of impact organizations around the world, and there are too many to name here. When you hear that India, for example, has more than three million NGOs, the vast majority of these are community-based ones."[4]

"I'm starting to understand the difference between them now," said Kim.

"Keep going with the turning points," Farah pressed.

"After World War II," Roshan continued, "humanity was entering a new area and needed new ways of solving problems.

---

4 "Rise of Third Sector," Down to Earth, accessed July 31, 2011, https://www.downtoearth.org.in/coverage/rise-of-third-sector-33712.

The traumatic world wars had shown that it was no longer possible for individual nations to deal with global problems; new global alliances were necessary. In parallel, decolonization movements succeeded all over the world, and many new countries officially came into being. All that led to the founding of the United Nations in 1945, with the mission to maintain international peace and security, develop friendly relations between nations, and promote social progress, better living standards, and human rights. The United Nations (UN) system is made up of not only the 193 member states, but also many programs, funds, and specialized agencies like UN Development Programme (UNDP), UN Children's Fund (UNICEF), UN Women, UN Refugee Agency (UNHCR), and several others."

Ilaina interjected, "This **rise of cooperation for international development**, created a whole new industry of impact-first jobs, not just in United Nations agencies, but also with the creation of other multilateral and government aid agencies. To start with, *multilateral agencies* are organizations created and funded by coalitions of governments to address common global issues beyond the scope of any one country, like poverty, women's rights, or climate change. Examples of well-known multilateral agencies include United Nations agencies, the World Bank Group, regional agencies like the African Union, or the Organisation for Economic Co-operation and Development (OECD), and regional financers such as the Asian Development Bank, among many others.

"In addition to these, there are also separate *government aid agencies*, created and funded by individual governments, usually from high-income countries, that provide bilateral development aid to low-income countries. More than forty countries have aid agencies."

"That many!" Farah sounded surprised.

"Yes," said Ilaina. "Examples of government aid agencies include the U.S. Agency for International Development (USAID), UK Aid Direct, (formerly DFID), Japan International Cooperation Agency (JICA), Germany's Deutsche Gesellschaft für Internationale Zusammenarbeit (GIZ), and Australian Aid."

"If I want to fight climate change, which is a big global challenge, then I should probably work with a multilateral agency," Kim said reflectively.

"Sure, but you also have other options brought about by the next turning point, the **rise of social entrepreneurship and social business**," noted Ilaina.

Roshan continued, "In the early 1980s, an American visionary named Bill Drayton, who had previously worked in both the public and private sectors, launched a new organization called Ashoka to support what he called 'innovators for the public.' In doing so, he kick-started the field that is now called social entrepreneurship. If you have ever seen this term in a news article or taken a class in university that dealt with this term, it is because of Ashoka."

In their different worlds, both Kim and Farah had heard about social entrepreneurship before.

"Even though I've heard about it, I've seen it used to describe different things," Kim said. "Can you explain it again?"

Roshan nodded. "Yes, there are many competing definitions out there. The one that we like defines a social entrepreneur as someone who 'targets an unfortunate [reality] that causes the...suffering of a segment of humanity; who brings to bear [entrepreneurial skills such as] inspiration, direct action, creativity, courage, and fortitude; and who aims for the establishment of a new equilibrium [that] benefits...society at large.'[5] Basically, the primary contribution made by social entrepreneurship has been to introduce innovation and entrepreneurship as key ingredients to the solving of social problems.

"It's important to note that the organizations founded by social entrepreneurs may be nonprofit or for-profit, or even a blend of both. Some of these organizations are called social businesses (also called social enterprises), and they aim to tackle social problems through the sale of goods or services that can be used to improve quality of life or reduce suffering. They prioritize social impact over financial returns.

---

5   Roger L. Martin and Sally Osberg, "Social Entrepreneurship: The Case for Definition," *Stanford Social Innovation Review*, Spring 2007, https://ssir.org/articles/entry/social_entrepreneurship_the_case_for_definition#.

"What Ashoka kicked off in the early 1980s was picked up over the next twenty years by many influential academics and philanthropists—like Jeff Skoll, one of the founders of eBay, and Klaus Schwab of the World Economic Forum, to name just two who created major foundations named after themselves to promote social entrepreneurship. Today, there are social entrepreneurs leading fabulous organizations to deal with pretty much every single social problem facing humanity.

"To illustrate with just one issue, let's take eye care or vision impairment. The Aravind Eye Care System in India is a social enterprise that today conducts more eye surgeries than any private hospital in the world, and yet they provide free surgeries for the poor and allow the rich to pay whatever they can. This model has influenced eye care for the poor all around the world. Another example is the Dialogue in the Dark museums, which aim to build empathy for the lives of blind people. If you ever have a chance to visit a Dialogue in the Dark museum, it's an incredible experience! This too has spread all around the world. And finally, there are several different organizations that have created innovative ways of providing free or very affordable spectacles to the poor. All these organizations are addressing just one issue (eye care) in one field (health). Multiply that across education, the environment, renewable energy, and other fields—and you can see the vast array of organizations that were spurred by Drayton's initial call to arms."

Ilaina took over.

"Once social entrepreneurship made clear that organizations solving social problems can also be structured as businesses, it was inevitable that people would wonder if one could generate social impact *as well as* financial returns to investors. Thus, a new actor appeared on the scene: impact investors, who fund social causes but expect a *return* on their investment, both in terms of getting their money back as well as seeing social impact. This marks the fifth turning point: **the rise of impact investing**.

"Acumen, a major impact investment fund, defines impact investing, or what it calls *patient capital*, as a form of funding that 'bridges the gap between the efficiency and scale of market-based approaches and the social impact of pure philanthropy. Patient capital has a high tolerance for risk, has long time horizons, is flexible to meet the needs of entrepreneurs, and is unwilling to sacrifice the needs of end customers for the sake of shareholders. At the same time, patient capital ultimately demands accountability in the form of a return of capital: proof that the underlying enterprise can grow sustainably in the long run.'[6]

"Today, impact investing is a $715 billion sector globally and is perhaps the fastest growing source of funding for the field of social impact.[7] It remains a relatively new field, and for every evangelist, there is a skeptic who doesn't believe in the possi-

---

6 "Patient Capital," Acumen, accessed July 13, 2021, https://acumen.org/about/patient-capital/.

7 Dean Hand, Hannah Dithrich, Sophia Sunderji, and Noshin Nova, *2020 Annual Impact Investor Survey*, Global Impact Investing Network, June 11, 2020, https://thegiin.org/research/publication/impinv-survey-2020.

bility of balancing financial and social returns. What's undeniable, however, is that impact investing is bringing previously untapped resources to the work of addressing social problems. Well-known impact investors besides Acumen include Village Capital, Omidyar Network, Intellecap, New Venture, and Fondo de EcoEmpresas.

"The rise of all these organizations working in social impact led to the **rise of intermediaries**, a further set of entities that don't work directly with needy populations but aim to build the capacity (financial or human or infrastructural or knowledge) of other organizations or individuals that do so. Intermediaries exist to support all the other kinds of organizations we've mentioned so far. They can be very action-oriented in terms of conducting training or building donation platforms or network ecosystems, or they can be more research-oriented, trying to understand what types of interventions work or what new problems may be arising in the world. Both the number and types of intermediaries are rising rapidly as the impact-first sector matures, with the increasing professionalization and specialization of the sector now requiring more varied kinds of supporting roles. Examples of intermediaries include the networks of social entrepreneurs we already mentioned like Ashoka and impact investors, but also charity: water, the Aspen Network of Development Entrepreneurs (ANDE), IDinsight, Abdul Latif Jameel Poverty Action Lab (J-PAL), Agora Partnerships and, of course, our very own Amani Institute!

"The world of management consulting was determined not to be left behind! Thus rose *Development Consulting Firms,* a type of intermediary that provides consulting services to government agencies, multilaterals, foundations, investors, and large NGOs. They too can be either nonprofit or for-profit in terms of legal structure. In fact, many large and famous management consulting firms now have social impact practices including Accenture, Boston Consulting Group, Deloitte, and McKinsey & Company. Other global examples include TechnoServe, Dalberg, Management Systems International, and Bridgespan."

Kim drained the rest of his drink. "I might need to order another!" he said. "There are just so many options, it's hard to keep track."

"Hang on just a bit more," said Ilaina. "We're almost there! When **Muhammad Yunus and Grameen Bank won the Nobel Peace Prize in 2006**, the world became aware of the role of microfinance in helping create a path out of poverty. Microfinance, launched by the Grameen Bank in 1983, is a category of financial services that helps individuals and small businesses who cannot access conventional banking services. Muhammad Yunus's work with the Grameen Bank inspired many other microfinance institutions around the world and raised the hope of lifting millions of people out of poverty. Today, that hope is dimmed by the many controversies it has given rise to, such as ethical dilemmas over the appropriateness of making profit off the poor and disagreements about what is a fair interest rate for them. But despite these controversies, microfinance made an essential contribution by changing the way we see the poor—not as helplessly awaiting handouts, but as active agents of their own empowerment, especially the role of women as credit-worthy leaders of upward mobility.

"While microfinance institutions primarily offer loans to low-income people, they may also offer financial products relating to specific needs such as insurance, health, energy, education, etc. Examples include Kiva, Pro Mujer, Root Capital, Opportunity International, and Accion."

"And then," Roshan continued, "we have the seventh turning point, the **rise of conscious capitalism**, which means that businesses must consider all major stakeholders when making decisions—not just customers and investors, but also their employees, the communities they operate in, their suppliers, and the environment as well. Conscious capitalism is sometimes referred to as 'shared value' or 'the triple bottom line.' It also gave rise to certification processes such as the growing B Corps movement.

"By redefining the role of business as a force for good and part of the solution, not just as a source of funds or as a source of problems that the social sector needs to fix, conscious capitalism marks an important turning point in the impact sector. Historically, the social sector and the private sector have viewed each other with a little bit of suspicion. Social impact professionals often stereotype the private sector as being the source of social problems, callous toward people negatively affected by their business, uncaring about environmental damage, and motivated only by making money. Likewise, private sector professionals can regard the social sector as being the source of higher costs on their business, intellectually 'less than' they are, and lacking the skills to do the 'real' work of creating economic value. Mistrust, accusations of impropriety, and dislike flew in both directions through most of the twentieth century.

"Over the last two decades, however, the tide has started to turn, increasingly gathering momentum as each side begins to view the other not (just) as an adversary, but also as a potential partner in creating win-win outcomes."

Ilaina jumped back in. "This brought new job opportunities for people seeking impact-first careers. First came *corporate social responsibility (CSR)*, in which private companies give away a portion of their profits. This usually takes the form of donations to local organizations working with needy populations. They can be either purely charitable or strategic in their giving. But then companies began to create their own *corporate foundations*, funded by the company but structured as a separate entity, through which they either fund other organizations or run their own programs to contribute to society. Examples of companies with a CSR department or corporate foundation include Nike, IKEA, Microsoft, LEGO, Fundación Telefónica, and The Tata Trusts. While some of these CSR departments and foundations are huge themselves, they were only the opening salvo from the private sector.

"Some leaders began to urge companies to rethink the very purpose of business itself. To some extent, this should not be surprising. As far back as the nineteenth century, Jamsetji Tata, the founder of India's largest conglomerate company, the Tata Group, proclaimed that the 'community is not just another stakeholder in a business but the very purpose of its existence.' And small businesses everywhere have always been invested in ensuring that their localities thrive. As we come into the modern era, however, it becomes even clearer that businesses cannot trample on the needs of the communities and environment in which they operate if they hope to be successful in the long term. And so, the doctrine of shareholder primacy and the pressure on quarterly earnings that dominated business thinking through the last quarter of the twentieth century is now often seen as too short-sighted a view of the role of business. For example, Edward Freeman, one of the original thought leaders of the conscious capitalism movement, famously said: 'We need red blood cells to live (the same way a business needs profits to live); but the purpose of life is more than to make red blood cells, the same way the purpose of business is more than simply to generate profits.'"[8]

"But isn't that just public relations talk? Does seeing business as a force for good actually help the bottom line of these companies?" countered Farah. "I can't imagine some of the companies I've worked for adopting these ideas!"

"This might surprise you, but this mindset actually helps companies too," said Roshan. "Companies that clearly define and communicate how they create value in society often actually end up delivering profits at or above the industry average.

---

8 "Conscious Capitalism Exists to Elevate Humanity," Conscious Capitalism, accessed July 13, 2021, https://www.consciouscapitalismchicago.org/Conscious-Capitalism.

It's not just the right thing to do, but it also leads to better business performance.[9] And that's not surprising, since job motivation is correlated with increased productivity and lower attrition rates. If companies have a clear purpose and employees find that purpose truly meaningful, they are often willing to trade money for that sense of meaning (i.e., accept lower salaries) and are more likely to remain passionate about what they do and loyal to the company. It's a win for the employee, for the company, and for the society at large.[10]

"In fact, at the start of 2019, Larry Fink, the CEO of BlackRock, the world's largest investment management company, wrote that a higher purpose than making money must be the 'engine of long-term profitability.' This caused quite a stir—when the world's largest money manager talks, people tend to listen. In 2020, Fink doubled down on his previous letter when he

---

9 PwC, *Our Research on the Connection between Strategic Purpose and Motivation*, accessed July 13, 2021, https://www.strategyand.pwc.com/gx/en/unique-solutions/capabilities-driven-strategy/approach/research-motivation.html. A study by global consulting giant PwC found that at companies that have clearly defined and communicated how they create value in society, 63 percent of employees say they're motivated, versus 31 percent at other companies; 65 percent say they're passionate about their work, versus 32 percent at other companies; and perhaps most tellingly, more than 90 percent of these companies deliver growth and profits at or above the industry average.

10 Shawn Achor, Andrew Reece, Gabriella Rosen Kellerman, and Alexi Robichaux, "9 Out of 10 People are Willing to Earn Less Money to Do More-Meaningful Work," *Harvard Business Review*, November 6, 2018, https://hbr.org/2018/11/9-out-of-10-people-are-willing-to-earn-less-money-to-do-more-meaningful-work. A study published in the *Harvard Business Review* surveyed the experience of workplace meaning among 2,285 American professionals, across twenty-six industries and a range of pay levels, company sizes, and demographics. They found that more than 90 percent of employees are willing to trade a percentage of their lifetime earnings for greater meaning at work; highly meaningful work will generate an additional $9,078 per worker, per year; and employees who find work meaningful are 69 percent less likely to plan on quitting their jobs within the next six months.

wrote that 'every government, company and shareholder must confront climate change.' In 2021, he continued his crusade, shrewdly noting how sustainable funds outperformed the market even during the downturn caused by the COVID-19 pandemic."[11]

Kim perked up at this. "This sounds promising, but do you think this trend will actually stick?"

"Well," Roshan continued, "all these are positive indicators that we are moving in the right direction. For instance, in August 2020, a coalition of CEOs of major multinational companies from companies like Danone, Mastercard, Philips, L'Oréal, and others signed on to a roadmap to build a more inclusive and sustainable post-COVID economy, with a special focus on recognizing and uplifting 'purpose-first' businesses.[12] And after Fink's 2021 letter, which focused on climate change, several big companies announced ambitious new goals—to name just two, Microsoft and Delta Airlines both said they plan to be carbon-neutral by 2030.[13]

"Change of this magnitude will happen slowly, but some businesses are already walking this talk. Lara Bezerra, the former

---

11 Andrew Ross Sorkin, "BlackRock Chief Pushes a Big New Climate Goal for the Corporate World," *The New York Times*, January 26, 2021, https://www.nytimes.com/2021/01/26/business/dealbook/larry-fink-letter-blackrock-climate.html.

12 Meridian, *Open Letter: Global Leadership COVID-19 Response,* August 2020, https://www.meridian.org/wp-content/uploads/2020/08/Global-Leadership-COVID-19-Response-Letter_Designed-v.12.pdf.

13 Sorkin, "BlackRock."

head of Roche Pharma's operations in India changed her title from Managing Director to Chief Purpose Officer. The famous outdoor clothing brand Patagonia has always been on the forefront of this movement, even making it explicit in their mission statement that they are in business to solve the environmental crisis facing humanity today. Look around and you will see plenty more examples like this.

"These developments are good news for you and all those who want to make impact in their careers since there will be new job opportunities in the private sector that are explicitly about having social impact. Living up to their values and purpose will mean that companies have to make progress toward greater inclusion and diversity, greater environmental sustainability, and perhaps even developing new products and services to foster cleaner energy, more affordable healthcare, access to credit, and so on."

Ilaina added, with a reassuring smile, "With the private sector joining the fray of social impact, a whole new world opens up where people can have an impact with their careers. This is one of the reasons we are sure the great majority of the jobs in the future will be impact-first."

"And now the last turning point," said Roshan. "When Bill and Melinda Gates partnered with legendary investor Warren Buffett in 2010 to create **The Giving Pledge**, a commitment by many of the world's wealthiest individuals to give away more than 50 percent of their wealth toward philanthropy, they kicked off a new era in philanthropy (thus bringing our evolution story full-circle), which today counts more than two hundred of the world's wealthiest people, from twenty-three countries."[14]

Kim whistled. "That's insane!"

Farah shrugged, looking unimpressed. "Being the richest people on the planet, surely they can do more to change the rules of the global economic system—more than just giving money away..."

"True, but they could also choose not to donate at all," Roshan responded. "However, it's interesting to notice who now has the money to change the world. For example, the endowment of the Bill & Melinda Gates Foundation in 2018 was $46.8 billion.[15] By contrast, the budget for the United Nations was a mere $5.4 billion.[16] And, these 2018 numbers represented an *increase* in the disparity from the start of the decade—the corresponding figures for 2012 were $31 billion for the Gates Foundation and $5.5 billion for the United Nations.

---

14   "History of the Pledge," The Giving Pledge, accessed July 13, 2021, https://givingpledge.org/About.aspx.

15   "Foundation Fact Sheet," Bill & Melinda Gates Foundation, accessed July 13, 2021, https://www.gatesfoundation.org/Who-We-Are/General-Information/Foundation-Factsheet.

16   United Nations, "Fifth Committee Recommends $5.4 Billion Budget for 2018-2019 Biennium as It Concludes Main Part of Seventy-Second Session," news release no. GA/AB/4270, December 23, 2017, https://www.un.org/press/en/2017/gaab4270.doc.htm.

"The influence of The Giving Pledge on many of the richest people in the world will bring a massive influx of funding to grow the impact sector significantly. That said, there are deeper questions to be asked when a small group of people can spend more money to shape the world than entire governments can.

"In our eyes, these eight developments represent the key turning points that have led to the new reason to work: impact!" Roshan finished.

"I see it now," said Kim. "Each of the turning points you described resulted in more and more impact-first job opportunities. And in more recent years, increasing numbers of traditional jobs have also started to turn into impact-first jobs. That's quite a liberating thought."

"Seeing this through the arc of history has been fascinating, but if I were to summarize in the present, I might say that there are four main groups of impact-first organizations today," Farah said, looking up from the notes she had been making during the conversation. "These would be: firstly, *NGOs or nonprofits*, comprising all the various kinds of NGOs you mentioned; second, *funding organizations*, comprising philanthropists, corporate foundations, CSR, impact investors, and microfinance institutions; thirdly, *support organizations*, comprising the wide range of intermediaries; and finally, *social businesses and traditional businesses* that are re-purposing toward impact. Does that make sense?"

"Sure!" Roshan said, nodding.

"This may be a tangent," Kim began, "but last weekend I participated in a protest march against the government's latest decision to allow coal mining to continue despite the damage to the environment. There were so many people there in support of fighting climate change. But I don't see that type of work included in your list of types of organizations."

"That's a great question, actually," Roshan said. "We should also be clear on what we have *not included* here. When we talk about impact-first careers, we are excluding what are typically called social movements. Social movements have existed for a very long time, of course, and still do, as seen in recent popular movements such as Black Lives Matter and #metoo.

"These tend to focus on what are considered, in the West at least, to be universal human rights. They encompass historic campaigns such as the abolition of slavery, decolonization and independence struggles, women's suffrage, the civil rights movement in the United States, anti-apartheid, gay rights, land rights, disability rights, and so on. However, there are many other types of social impact movements as well. A few examples could include movements for public benefit (banning smoking in public places or drunk driving), peace (anti-nuclear proliferation, anti-war, anti-landmines), economic justice (the World Social Forum or Occupy Wall Street), and conscious consumerism (banning plastic bags, promoting vegetarianism, recycling, and so on).

"These movements have been *essential* throughout history to move the human race forward to becoming better versions of ourselves. We wholeheartedly endorse and celebrate when citizens voluntarily get together to collectively improve the state of the world. However, our topic here is the professional realm. You cannot get a job with Black Lives Matter or with promoting recycling. But you *can* get a job with a nonprofit dedicated to improving civil rights or a social enterprise that organizes a better recycling system in a city. Movements transcend professions—they do not give you a career."

HOW TO DECIDE WHICH TYPE OF IMPACT-FIRST CAREER IS FOR YOU

We completed our meals and the waitress cleared our plates. As we settled our bill, Kim shook his head. "I hate to say this, but I'm even more confused now that I have a whole universe of organizations to pick from! I now see that I can work on climate change in so many more organizations than I first thought. However, I still don't know how to decide among them all."

Farah backed him up. "Just knowing the options for organizations where you can work is eye-opening, but it isn't enough. There really is a vast set of options for working in social impact. You talked about organizational structures, but you didn't give us a cause or issue breakdown such as organizations working in education, healthcare, renewable energy, environmental conservation, and so on."

"You're right," Ilaina said. "And even more than that, this is just a snapshot in time today. With constant innovations in business models, legal frameworks, and pure human ingenuity, the range of organizations is only likely to increase in the years to come.

"Therefore, the next step is to ask yourself six critical questions to help you narrow down your opportunities from among all of these types of organizations.

"The first question to ask yourself is: **how important is it for you to interact directly with the beneficiaries of your work**? If you want to save lives, your best option is to work within humanitarian NGOs, since they are tangibly and viscerally about saving life. If you don't need to save lives directly but still want to visibly see the impact you are making, development NGOs and local nonprofits and community-based organizations are great options, since you will work closely with communities. Depending on the role you have, social businesses can also be a good way to work in the field. You get further away from the field and from seeing a tangible impact when you work with human rights NGOs, since their work is usually around political advocacy, and you get even further away when choosing foundations, intermediaries, and most multilateral or government aid agencies. The less you focus on a specific community or problem and the more you focus on solving the systemic cause of the problem, the less you will work directly with beneficiaries and the more your impact will be indirect and less tangible, even though it may actually result in larger-scale change.

"We find that the choices people make here are often directly related to their personality—some people really enjoy being in close contact with the communities they are helping, and others are better suited to an office environment working toward macro solutions. However, both types of work are equally valuable and complement each other! We recommend that every impact-first professional gets experience at both levels before deciding where their interests and skills are best deployed.

"Then, ask yourself **how important is your net income (salary and benefits) and lifestyle**? If a high salary and/or a clear career ladder to climb are very important to you, then you should consider multilateral agencies, government aid agencies, corporations, and development consulting firms a lot more than you would look at local nonprofits and community-based organizations. Some multilateral agencies even provide a tax-free income! On the other hand, small NGOs find it hard to pay competitive salaries or build a structured career ladder for their staff. Larger NGOs and most social businesses usually offer poor salaries at junior levels but generally do better at middle and senior roles.

"Another important question is: **how dedicated are you to a particular cause or geographic location**? If you, like Kim currently is with climate change, are fired up to work on a particular issue or a specific city or country, then you might consider a social business or development NGO, local nonprofit or community-based organization, or a foundation or impact investment firm that is working on that issue or location. By contrast, if you prefer to work on many different projects across multiple fields, countries, and sectors, you might consider humanitarian NGOs, development consulting firms, or intermediaries. Of course, human rights NGOs and microfinance institutions are self-explanatory in this regard.

"Also, ask yourself: **what type of organizational culture and work environment do I prefer**? The impact of an organization's culture on employee job satisfaction has become increasingly apparent. For example, autonomy is one crucial motivational factor that most young people demand these days. Different types of organizations provide varying levels of autonomy or freedom when it comes to daily work. Multilateral agencies, government aid agencies and international NGOs tend to be rather bureaucratic and slow-moving and offer little freedom to innovate. Human rights NGOs and development NGOs in general are highly dependent on their donors' priorities in terms of what type of work they can and cannot take on. However, it is also fair to say that both humanitarian NGOs and development NGOs are showing an increased interest in social innovation in order to improve their work and are starting to diversify their revenue sources.

"On the other hand, local nonprofits, social businesses, and intermediaries typically offer much more flexibility and freedom to innovate and a flatter organizational hierarchy. This is especially true of social businesses and intermediaries that do not depend on donors to be financially sustainable.

"Another important cultural factor could be how your work affects other parts of your life. Development consulting firms usually have long workdays, extended periods of time away from home and family, and competitive work cultures. Many multilateral agencies, government aid agencies, humanitarian NGOs, and foundations also require a lot of international travel. This, of course, is highly attractive to some employees and a deal-breaker for others who may have valid reasons not to travel. Some jobs, especially in humanitarian NGOs, could involve significant exposure to death, war, injury, sexual violence, corruption, physical destruction, and so on, making them both physically dangerous and emotionally hazardous, depending on the nature of emergency. Working at a human rights NGO can also be physically dangerous depending on local politics.

"Next up, you must ask yourself **whether you prefer to manage, research, fundraise, advocate, or implement projects**. In general, all organizations require these types of activities, but different types of organizations do them to different extents. If your thing is advocacy, then consider human rights NGOs or some jobs at multilateral agencies and government aid agencies. If you like fundraising, then you will always have a job at any kind of NGO! If you want to directly implement long-term projects, then development NGOs, local nonprofits, or social businesses are for you. If you're the analytical type who loves research, then development consulting, impact investing, multilateral agencies, and government aid agencies all provide plenty of opportunities to do so.

"The sixth important question is: **what kind of organizations do your previous education and professional experiences set you up for**? As a rule of thumb, the larger the organization, the more conventional it is regarding educational backgrounds. Most mid- and senior-level jobs at multilateral organizations, government aid agencies, human rights NGOs, and large development NGOs will require a master's degree from a reputed university and sometimes even a PhD. Development consulting firms, microfinance institutions, and impact investors will often look for the quantitative and finance skills that come with an MBA degree or a public policy degree from a major university, and/or prior work experience in corporate finance or management consulting. By contrast, your educational background matters less when it comes to social businesses and local nonprofit organizations—these organizations are usually more interested in your history of commitment to the cause and previous professional experiences. These are, of course, general rules, and there are real-life exceptions to all of them," Ilaina finished, almost out of breath.

"Could you give us an example of someone who had to wrestle with these questions during their career?" Farah asked.

"I'll tell you about a Brazilian friend, Celia Cruz," Roshan began. "Celia's thirty-year career has spanned many of the types of organizations we've discussed. She began her career in the private sector, like you Farah. While working at IBM, she realized the importance, for her, of being passionate about her work—and she just wasn't passionate about selling computers. She left IBM to pursue a master's degree, which took her to Europe, India, Nepal, and Canada. On returning to Brazil, she began working as a fundraising consultant, a skill she had picked up doing internships with local nonprofits in Canada. In other words, she became an intermediary, helping nonprofits raise money. She has largely stayed in the intermediary sector ever since, apart from a few years with a large community development NGO. Yet, she has had diverse experiences within intermediaries: after several years as a fundraiser, she spent a decade building Ashoka's network of social entrepreneurs in Brazil, and she has spent the past decade developing Brazil's impact investing ecosystem through an organization called Instituto de Cidadania Empresarial (ICE).

"As you can see, Celia has worked in companies, local nonprofits, NGOs, and various kinds of intermediaries. In the future, she is keen to foster conscious capitalism, helping large companies become more impact-first. But to return to the six questions that help you decide your career choices, the reason Celia has spent most of her career with intermediaries is that she realized as early as high school, through supporting local nonprofits in Brazil, that she is better suited to organizational or ecosystem-level work. She gets too emotionally affected when working directly with suffering people. She is also more engaged by working systemically across many different issues, rather than focusing on just one cause. Her educational background in economics trained her to see issues in a systemic way, which fits her inclination toward intermediary work. And while she has enjoyed working in North America and partnering with colleagues across the world, she feels most invested in her home country of Brazil. In terms of organizational culture, Celia is a born innovator, so she loves the autonomy, flatter hierarchies, and space to experiment that she has found in intermediaries like Ashoka and ICE. Finally, in terms of her salary, she's always just wanted to cover her family's costs, especially toward her kids' education. Now that her sons are off to university, she sees herself accepting lower salaries as she advances in her career."

"Thanks for a lovely evening, but now it's quite late!" Ilaina said. "We better get going!"

"Oh no, I don't want the evening to end!" Farah exclaimed. "Celia's story was inspiring, and I'm getting so many ideas for my own career through those six questions. But I still have so much to ask you! Can we please meet again?"

Kim joined in. "There really is a whole universe of options out there, and I feel it's critical to reflect carefully about how to build the skills I need and to understand what I really want to do. Will you help me with that?"

"All right," Ilaina said. "But you first need to do some home-work, if you're up for it."

"Yes, that would help me get started," said Farah, with Kim nodding enthusiastically beside her.

When everyone sat down again around the table, Roshan said, "Answering the questions we just asked is valuable because each of us differs in what is most important. A feature that may be a *pro* to one person, such as working directly with benefi-ciaries or the requirement for international travel, may well be a *con* to another whose skills are more suited for office-based work or who cannot travel for family reasons. It's important to find what *you* are best suited for.

"As homework then, you will first identify variables that help you pick a type of organization. Identify up to ten crite-ria! For example: working directly with beneficiaries, work-ing at the systems/macro level, remuneration, flexibility, space to innovate, a clear career trajectory, travel, and so on. Once your list is ready, rank your variables from one to five. Choosing a one will mean *not important at all,* while a five will mean *non-negotiable.* Once you've ranked the variables, pick two to three *types* of organizations that best fit your criteria, based on our conversation tonight. You can supplement your analysis by researching some of the actual organizations we mentioned today.

"Once you're done, contact us and we can meet again to go over it. And now, we should really get going!"

ACTION AND REFLECTION

Act:

1. Would you say that you are closer to Kim's career stage or to Farah's? Keep that answer in mind for the rest of the book.

2.   Identify three *types* of impact-first organizations that
     most interest you given your background and profes-
     sional interests. Then do the exercise described at the
     end of the chapter to help you decide which ones to
     pursue.

3.   Most of the general public isn't aware of the wide
     range of impact-first organizations today. Share your
     new knowledge with a few people who would benefit
     from it.

Reflect:

1.   Which of the turning points described above most
     surprised you, and why?

2.   Were any of the types of impact-first organizations
     new to you? Why might you have not heard of them
     before?

PART II

SIX "KEYS" TO UNLOCK YOUR OWN IMPACT-FIRST CAREER

3

DESIGNING YOUR OWN EDUCATION

WHERE TRADITIONAL EDUCATION DOESN'T HELP

Two weeks later, we received an email from Kim and Farah: "We did our homework, and we're ready to meet again."

We gathered online a few days later, our thumbnail images filling laptop screens. We could see that Farah looked calm, but Kim looked worried. He was the first to speak: "I know where I want to work, but I've been looking at job postings, and I do not have the skills needed. I don't feel prepared for the kinds of jobs I want."

"You're reminding me of something that happened a few years ago," said Roshan. "I was at a party to celebrate thirty years of

Ashoka, the organization where we used to work. The celebration happened at a two-hundred-year-old imperial dance hall in Paris. The walls were covered in red velvet and gold leaves. It was after midnight, and most of us were many drinks in. A short-haired, middle-aged Mexican woman danced up to me and gave me a big hug. I gave her a long hug back, because seeing her was one of the highlights of my professional life. In the previous two years, I'd spent many hours on the phone with her, helping her think through life and death choices. *Her* life and death.

"She was a soldier in the long battle to prevent the trafficking of women and girls. As such, she lived under constant physical threat from Mexico's trafficking cartels. She described the point-blank assassinations of acquaintances in broad daylight and the attempts on her own life. We talked about her choices to stay safe. For example, should she hide from the mafia or get even more public? If she hid, and they found her, it would be easy to kill her in secret. If she became even more public, she'd be easier to find, but at least it raised the stakes of going after her.

"'What should I do?' she asked me. Safe and sound in my twentieth-floor office, overlooking the sights of beautiful Washington, DC, I felt very far away from the Mexican underworld. I stared into her image on the Skype window, my heart full of dread and my mind utterly empty. I had no idea what to tell her.

"As wonderful as it was to see her there in Paris, dancing with the joy of being alive, I also remembered how impotent I had felt on the Skype call because I didn't know how to help her, even though I've been privileged enough to have a fantastic education. And in a career working in social entrepreneurship across five continents, I had known that sinking feeling over and over again. My education had not prepared me for the work I had to do."

"But what education could possibly prepare you to advise someone in the crosshairs of a mafia?" Farah exclaimed, throwing her hands up in the air.

"Actually, there's a set of skills that would have helped Roshan support that Mexican changemaker. Skills like active listening, empathy, coaching, and so on," replied Ilaina.

Roshan nodded. "But I had never been taught any of these skills, whether in school, university, or graduate studies. And yet, these are skills that may have made a difference not only in that life-and-death situation, but also in many types of everyday office interactions. I had to learn them on the job."

THE KEY SKILLS FOR IMPACT-FIRST CAREERS

"Thanks for sharing this story, Roshan!" said Kim. "But are you saying the skills I learned at university are not enough to get an impact-first job? I am now even more worried than I was at the start of this meeting. My parents sacrificed a lot to send me to college. Please don't tell me it was all in vain."

Farah interjected, empathetically. "I am really sorry Kim, but considering my experience, I think they are right. Most of the skills I needed to advance my career, I didn't get at university. I guess that is also true about working toward impact."

"Unfortunately, Farah is right," responded Ilaina. "Society demands too much from universities these days: to be repositories and generators of knowledge, to provide skills for employment, to be at the cutting-edge of innovation and technology, to influence public discourse, and more. That's too much for one institution to take on. Historically, the purpose of universities has been the pursuit of knowledge for its own sake—and they're good at that. But universities were never meant to prepare people for professional careers, let alone solve global problems. Social change is about action, not just critical thinking and knowledge acquisition. To change the world, you need much more than your university can provide.

"If you want to be an impact-first professional, you must understand that academic study is not sufficient preparation for employment. You must supplement your formal education. But it's not too late! The good news—for you and your parents—is that doing so will be way cheaper than university!"

Kim started to look less downcast, his upbeat personality already reasserting itself. "Then tell me how universities are failing to properly prepare graduates for impact-first careers. And what are the skills most in demand by impact-first employers?"

"That was the question that kick-started our journey toward creating Amani Institute," Roshan replied. "To find an answer, we interviewed leaders of several major social impact organizations. One of the most revealing questions you can ask an employer is what makes their best employees a cut above the rest. And similarly, ask them what makes someone an especially disappointing employee. Let me share a couple of the responses we got," said Roshan while looking at some documents on his computer. "Here!" he said, sharing his screen.

"According to Eric Glustrom, the founder and CEO of Watson Institute, which aims to accelerate the careers of entrepreneurial youth, 'Versatility, especially in young organizations, is [incredibly valuable]. There is a great need to focus on recruiting staff one day, then leading Monitoring and Evaluation the next day. Also, comfort with uncertainty—in our work, goals, and the situation around us—knowing that it is the clay out of which progress is molded.'[17]

"On the other side of the coin, Vishal Talreja, co-founder of Dream a Dream, an incredible nonprofit in India that helps youth from vulnerable backgrounds build the abilities to thrive in the modern world, reflected: 'My most disappointing hires were those who were always coming up with reasons for why something won't work, or waiting to be told what needs to be done instead of [having an attitude of] achieving the goal.'[18]

---

17 Roshan Paul and Ioana Tesliuc, "The State of Talent Development in the Social Sector," The Amani Institute, January 2013, https://amaniinstitute.org/wp-content/uploads/2016/08/State-of-Talent-Development-in-the-Social-Sector-Final-w-cover-2.pdf.

18 Ibid.

"Yet another inspirational leader, Shona McDonald, the founder of South Africa's Uhambo Foundation, which enables children with disability to lead full and happy lives, summed it up nicely when she said, 'We need people to have the desire and willingness to use their skills and energy to positively influence [change].'"[19]

When Roshan stopped sharing his screen, Farah was first to comment, running her hands through her hair. "I notice that all those responses are about the employee *as a person.*"

"Yes," confirmed Ilaina. "For many employers in the impact-first sector, who a person *is* matters a great deal, at least as much as what they know and what they can do."

"But are there any *specific* skills that would be important for us to learn?" asked Kim expectantly, determination writ large on his face.

"Of course," Ilaina responded. "Over the past decade, several influential organizations have carefully studied what skills are needed as the global economy shifts over time, particularly given the coming age of artificial intelligence and what some call the 'fourth industrial revolution.'[20] When we polled employers all around the world on what skills are most in demand for making social impact, their answers nicely mirrored what all these studies were discovering. What high-performing professionals must be good at can be grouped into four 'buckets' of skills.

------

19 Ibid.

20 Ibid.

"Firstly, they need to have **innovation skills**—the ability to solve problems, create new possibilities, be creative in the face of adversity, manage uncertainty, design from the users' perspective, learn from multiple perspectives and sources, and apply that knowledge to the situation at hand. Secondly, there are **core leadership skills** that everyone can improve, both to manage oneself (understand how your preferences shape your actions, regulate your emotions, connect with your passion and use it as an enduring source of energy, take responsibility, be reli able, and stay positive in tough situations) as well as to inspire others (listen well, empathize, motivate, delegate, and build trust) toward a common goal. Third comes essential **communication skills** such as the ability to work in a team, public speaking, storytelling, facilitation, coaching, giving feedback, and so on. And the final bucket is **management skills** including the ability to run projects, negotiate win-win solutions, fundraise, measure social impact, satisfy all stakeholders, think systemically, possess basic financial literacy, and so on.

"We have trained more than ten thousand people all around the world in these skills and learned that they are indeed fundamentally important for being a high-quality professional in the twenty-first century. Furthermore, almost no one develops these skills during higher education, regardless of what type of education they have had or where they come from. And while you can become good at each of these skills over time, you can never fully master them. Even Barack Obama had a team of speechwriters. There is always value in brushing up on these skills throughout your career, learning and applying the latest techniques, and practicing constantly."

Kim interrupted, sounding a bit peeved. "But I *did* learn some of those skills at university."

"I'm sure you did, but mostly they fall out of the purview of what universities cover," said Roshan. "Think about the primary 'user interface' of university education: you read a lot, listen to lectures, and then make arguments on paper directly to your professor. Most real-world work does not happen this way. You typically collaborate with others, manage projects, make presentations, and so on. All this while keeping a close watch on your own preferences, energy, motivation, and habits."

WHERE TECHNICAL SKILLS COME IN

"Besides innovation, leadership, management, and communication, are there more technical skills that we must learn, or are those simply not important?" asked Kim.

"There are certainly useful technical skills!" Roshan admitted. "We aren't claiming that technical skills are unimportant, but rather that they are overvalued in both the education industry as well as traditional recruitment processes, and are not as career-determining as soft skills. Having some hard skills certainly helps you apply for specific roles. You will find opportunities to work in social impact if you possess any of the following skills: professional writing, applied research, video production (filming, editing, producing), graphic design, data analysis and visualization, financial management and accounting, social media, logistics, project management, supply chain management, nutrition, engineering, law, and an affinity for new technologies like virtual reality, artificial intelligence, blockchain, and so on.

"This is certainly not an exhaustive list. The social sector is vast, and different problems require different kinds of expertise. The trick is how you apply these skills to the cause of solving social problems."

Farah's face lit up. "I'm relieved to know I can use my graphic design skills for social impact."

"Indeed," responded Roshan with a smile, "you just need to apply them differently."

HOW TO DESIGN YOUR OWN EDUCATION, PART ONE

A Different Approach to Learning

Kim unmuted himself and said: "This is where it gets tricky. I understand what skills I need to make social change, but where do I learn them if not at university? And where do I practice them?"

We smiled at each other. Then Ilaina said: "And that was the second question we asked ourselves when starting Amani Institute! After a decade of testing out and continually refining different learning methodologies, we've concluded that there is no single place to learn the skills you need. Rather, there's a set of learning principles and methods to consider when acquiring the skills needed for an impact-first career."

"What are they?" asked Kim, practically glued to the screen.

"The first principle, **holistic learning**, comes from humanistic psychology," Ilaina replied. "It teaches that, to help people achieve their full potential, we must *consider the whole person*. Social impact work is very personal, so a whole-person approach means understanding that we're educating a human being with a body, thoughts, and emotions. This human also has a past, a present, and a vision for their future. They have a family, hobbies, motivations, and basic needs. When I was nineteen years old, I worked with the Argentine Youth Council, an institution that convenes and represents youth organizations in the region. Their office was in Santiago de Compostela, Spain's Celtic-influenced town. Every morning, I walked through the ancient, winding, cobbled streets, thinking about my mission to develop young people as active citizens. I needed to learn how to manage European Union projects and organize transcontinental youth gatherings. I also had to get used to being away from my family, navigating a new culture, managing my emotions, and so on. If my manager hadn't understood and coached me on this, I wouldn't have done as well as I did."

Farah nodded. "When I go to tennis lessons, if I have not slept or eaten well, or I'm just having a bad day, my game suffers. Only when my coach understands my *holistic* situation are we able to improve my strokes."

"What is the next principle?" asked Kim, looking up from his notes.

Roshan continued, "The next one is **experiential learning**, which is the philosophy that adults learn techniques and skills *in the process of applying them in the real world*. Learning a skill through experience allows us to adapt it to different contexts and unknown scenarios. You want to be effective in the real world, with real people, so the more realistic the scenario where you apply the skills, the better you will learn them. For instance, you can understand how others have been great leaders by reading books and listening to professors, but the only way to truly learn to lead is by leading. It's like saying that you can master ocean swimming by reading a book, or watching a video, or even in a swimming pool. It is quite another thing to swim in the sea with ocean currents. Ilaina, why don't you tell them about your human resources story!"

"Sure," Ilaina said. "At the start of my career, I was nominated to the executive council of the Argentine Youth Organization for the United Nations, which promotes the values and policies of the United Nations in different countries. I was asked to lead the human resources department, even though I had no background in human resources. I had just finished high school! Welcome to the real world, I thought. So, I bought a standard handbook on human resources, and then just got started. For three years during university, I created and grew the human resources department of an organization with more than two hundred people across Argentina. I learned how to do it by trying things out in practice. For example, I developed a new national-level volunteer onboarding plan based on my own experience as a volunteer. After rolling it out once, we improved it based on the results and feedback from other volunteers, and the following year we improved it again."

Kim's image froze and then disappeared. Used to Wi-Fi connectivity issues, we just waited. Soon enough he was back, apologizing for his internet connection.

"No worries," said Ilaina. "I was about to describe the next principle: **challenge-based learning** or **the willingness to enter your stretch zone**. Karl Rohnke, an expert in experiential education, created the comfort/stretch/panic zone model. Have you heard of it?"

Kim and Farah shook their heads.

Ilaina continued. "Picture three concentric circles. The circle in the center is our comfort zone, where we do tasks that are familiar to us. We already have the skills and confidence to do them. The middle circle is our stretch zone, and this is where most of our learning happens. When we are learning a new skill, the stretch zone is where we confront and vanquish our own fears and self-doubts. It is challenging and exciting, and at times uncomfortable. Mihaly Csikszentmihalyi, a renowned psychologist, describes it as an experience when 'a person's body or mind is stretched to its limits in a voluntary effort to accomplish something difficult and worthwhile.'[21] Now, there

---

21 Mihaly Csikszentmihalyi, *Flow: The Psychology of Optimal Experience* (New York: HarperCollins, 2008).

may be times when what we are learning is too uncomfortable, almost unbearable. When this happens, we have entered the panic zone, the outermost of the three circles. In this zone, we experience stress and fear in such a way that it overwhelms our capacity to learn. We might need to change the method or the context in which the learning is happening.

"When learning a new skill, you need to locate yourself in the stretch zone. For each individual, the sizes and content of the zones are different. Your emotions will indicate which zone you are in. If you feel excitement and arousal, you are more likely to be in the stretch zone than if you start feeling bored or anxious. Roshan, you have a good example of this, don't you?"

"Indeed," said Roshan. "In 2008, I learned the storytelling techniques pioneered by Dr. Marshall Ganz at Harvard University, which were used to great effect in the Obama presidential campaign. After the election, Dr. Ganz would send out some of his former students, like me, to train various groups in these techniques. As I did so, I realized that they were equally valuable for leadership and management as for politics. To test out this hypothesis, I conducted a training course on storytelling at my then workplace. I had never run a full training by myself before, so I was totally in my stretch zone! But I worked hard to prepare the program, and it went very well. Soon I was doing workshops in many other places, including major universities and companies. In one case, I even traded my storytelling teaching skills for a scholarship worth more than $40,000 to attend a leadership program I could not otherwise afford. So that initial decision to put myself in the stretch zone to learn how to teach storytelling led to a wonderful series of benefits and a tangible new skill in training and facilitating. But once I had done more than a dozen of these workshops, and personally trained several hundred people, I realized it had now become part of my comfort zone. I actually became less interested in doing it anymore.

"This is an important thing to remember. Eventually, what's in your current stretch zone will move into your comfort zone and thus the boundaries of your comfort zone will push outward, thereby also pushing out your stretch and panic zones. What was previously in your panic zone will then move into your stretch zone, thus no longer a reason for panic. This is how you know without a doubt that your skills and capacities have increased!"

"When were you last in your stretch zone?" Ilaina asked Farah.

After some reflection, she responded, "While looking at the types of impact-first organizations I could work with, I realized that working in a corporate environment would be my comfort zone, while working abroad in an NGO would be in my stretch zone. However, my husband and I want to start a family and I am not sure it is the right moment to start a new career. The mere thought of it makes me anxious." She stopped to reflect further and then continued. "Maybe that would be my panic zone. My stretch zone could be working in an NGO, but in my own city."

"Each of us needs to understand our zones; no one can do that for us," responded Roshan. "And if you do work with an NGO anywhere, you will also experience the next learning principle: **contextual learning**. It's not just important to learn the skills experientially. *Where* you learn them also matters. For example, you can learn how to manage a team largely drawn from one ethnic group doing, say, financial analysis. But that's a far cry from managing a diverse team in a very different culture that is tasked to provide access to healthcare in a slum. It can also often be different within a corporate vis-à-vis an NGO. For example: how do you motivate team members in an NGO who didn't choose their jobs because of money? You can't just order them around because you are their boss, nor can you incentivize them through salary hikes (because you don't have that kind of money to throw at the problem and because you know that won't motivate them anyway).

"This also applies to technical skills. Let's take the example of a skill gaining importance for impact-first careers: data analysis, or the ability to see trends in data and draw conclusions from it. But if you do not understand the history and group dynamics of the organization you're in, you aren't able to understand the data in its specific context, or you aren't able to communicate the implications of the data compellingly or persuade your colleagues of its importance, then your expertise in data analysis won't serve you very well."

This resonated with Kim. "I did an on-campus job last semester, but only learned the skills in a university context and always felt uncertain about applying it anywhere else."

"What is the next principle?" asked Farah, trying to calm down her cat, which had climbed onto her lap and looked ready to jump onto her keyboard. We all laughed.

Ilaina, still laughing, continued. "That's a good segue to the next principle: **engagement-based learning**, which is about *making learning fun*. I grew up hearing my dad often say that 'the letter with blood enters.' As an adult, I learned that phrase was the title of a Francisco Goya masterpiece. Goya, a Spanish painter and printmaker, was critiquing the educational system of his time. The painting depicts a school in which the teacher is whipping a student whose buttocks are in the air, the student forced to bend over to receive punishment. Two other students have also just received the thrashing, while others are engrossed in their homework. Goya painted it in 1780, more than two centuries ago! Unfortunately, so many people still see learning as an exercise in suffering, with no space for fun. Yet we believe that having fun is an important element of learning."

Roshan snorted. "That's a great example of how education hasn't changed much through the centuries! I grew up in India with that kind of corporal punishment happening all the time. Fortunately, it's now largely been banned in India too, but it was still common in the 1990s."

"Wait, you actually got beaten in school?" Ilaina asked incredulously. "I didn't know that."

"One day my chemistry teacher literally kicked me in the ass in front of the whole class, just for borrowing a pen without asking him first," Roshan said, shaking his head at the memory.

"I still can't imagine adults learning through play and laughter. That's more for children, right?" inquired Farah.

"Not at all," Roshan responded. "Even in higher education, research shows that activities such as games (from sports to virtual to strategy games), role-playing activities, and simulations are very important. When integrating games into the learning process, you're aiming for three outcomes—cognitive, behavioral, and affective learning. Games are very effective at promoting knowledge acquisition as well as cognitive understanding. Regarding behavioral outcomes, games offer a plethora of learning opportunities by enhancing interaction and feedback among players, and developing soft skills like teamwork and collaboration. Regarding the affective domain, games can strongly influence students' motivation, engagement, and satisfaction.[22] Game-based courses in higher education have often led to higher enjoyment than non-game-based courses—and more enjoyment of a lesson correlates with improvements in deep learning. This is particularly important in situations where students are low in confidence and/or high in anxiety."[23]

"But isn't there a difference between playing and having fun?" asked a still-skeptical Kim.

---

22 Francesco Crocco, Kathleen Offenholley, and Carlos Hernandez, "A Proof-of-Concept Study of Game-Based Learning in Higher Education," *Simulation & Gaming* 47, no. 4 (August 2016): 403–422, https://doi.org/10.1177/1046878116632484.

23 Dimitrios Vlachopoulos *and* Agoritsa Makri, "The Effect of Games and Simulations on Higher Education: A Systematic Literature Review," *International Journal of Educational Technology in Higher Education* 14, no. 22 (2017) https://doi.org/10.1186/s41239-017-0062-1.

"Right," said Ilaina, "but laughing and having fun also have positive influences on learning! Humor helps students improve problem-solving, absorb and retain more information more quickly, and reduce anxiety.[24] And when the class is fun, attendance also increases.[25] At Amani Institute, we play a game called 'How Fascinating,' a very fun and insightful way for our students to internalize how essential the willingness to make mistakes and fail is to the innovation process. Even years after they've graduated, when our alumni meet and someone confesses to a mistake, everyone will often raise their hands in the air and exclaim at the same time, 'How fascinating!', which inevitably provokes nostalgic giggles.

"Finally, it's not all about doing things or having fun. Knowledge and experience alone do not necessarily lead to learning, and this is where the last learning principle, **reflective learning**, comes into play. Deliberate reflection is vital because it helps us consciously connect to our own experience—what we have heard, seen, done, and felt. Reflection allows ideas to connect and insights to crystallize to achieve a higher level of understanding. For example, if you are studying how to become a better manager while actively managing an organization, you better set aside time to reflect on how the theory comes alive in your daily work and how you can apply the new concepts you are learning. Only then will you become a better manager."

---

24 William B. Strean, "Evolving Toward Laughter in Learning," *Collected Essays on Learning and Teaching* 1, (2008): 77–81, https://doi.org/10.22329/celt.v1i0.3182.

25 Alan Seidman and Stephen C. Brown, "Laugh and Learn," *Adult Learning* 27, no. 1 (July 2015): 41–43, https://doi.org/10.1177/1045159515596160.

HOW TO DESIGN YOUR OWN EDUCATION, PART TWO

Getting the Skills to Thrive in Any Career

Kim reflected, "I get it. My university experience was great, but I didn't learn what I needed to create social impact. For that, I must put myself in real-life situations where the six principles you described come together, correct?"

METHODOLOGIES
to learn

- SEEK OUT ON-THE-JOB LEARNING EXPERIENCES
- START YOUR OWN PROJECT OR ORGANIZATION
- LEARN FROM AND WITH OTHERS
- IMMERSE YOURSELF INTO DIFFERENT PROJECTS

"Exactly!" said Ilaina. "Of course, you may have to combine more than one method to get the training you need. We will now share our four favorite ways to deploy these learning principles to acquire necessary skills. Are you ready to keep going?"

Farah responded with an emphatic nod. Kim clicked the button for the thumbs-up emoticon to pop up on all our screens.

"Great!" Roshan began. "Our favorite way to acquire skills for social impact is **on-the-job experiences** in which a person participates in actual tasks at a workplace. This can come through a formal job, an internship, an apprenticeship, or by volunteering. But while this is one of the most important ways to learn the skills you will need, it can also be one of the most challenging and frustrating ways, because it keeps you in the stretch zone for long periods, in a very holistic and experiential way. We know this from firsthand experience because we have carefully set up more than 350 internships for people from more than sixty-five countries with some of the most sought-after organizations in the social sector. To date, our Fellows have delivered more than one hundred thousand hours of work in social impact organizations."

"Impressive!" exclaimed Farah. "Can you give us some tips? How can we set up a successful on-the-job learning experience for ourselves?"

"That's a good question," said Roshan. "It's not enough to just find the organization to work, intern or volunteer. You also need to be intentional in your approach. Here are four tips to consider.

"First, it is essential to remember that *on-the-job experiences are about learning, not accomplishments*. Manage your expectations, because it's unlikely you will 'change the world' during this experience, particularly if it is an internship or volunteer experience. Focus on harvesting lessons and insights that will guide the rest of your career. Beyond specific skills, you will also learn more about yourself as a professional, about how social change actually happens in the world, the kinds of dysfunctions that exist in impact-first work, and whether you are able to accept working amid those dysfunctions in order to build a social impact career.

"Secondly, be conscious that a good experience is not always about picking a renowned organization to build your CV, but rather about *picking the right manager and tasks*. Before you start, you should ask what your tasks will be and who will manage you—those details can make the experience a success more than the 'brand' of the organization ever could. And, if you are clear on what you want to learn, you can share that with the organization so they can hopefully give you suitable tasks for your goal. As we will discuss later, having a mentor or role model is a great way to learn. Therefore, getting to know your manager and encouraging them to talk about their own career trajectories is also a good component of a successful experience.

"Third, take time to *really understand the organization*. One way to learn how the impact sector works is to truly understand the organization you are placed in, its history, accomplishments and failures, culture, future goals, and so on. Make the extra effort to do so, even if it is not required.

"Finally, *be patient and persistent!* If things don't go according to plan, then keep looking for other ways to make it valuable. As one of our mentors likes to say, when it comes to social impact, your work begins at 'No.'

"One of my favorite examples to illustrate these tips comes from the efforts of Joy Mwaniki, an Amani Fellow from Kenya. For her internship, we had matched Joy with an NGO that employed disadvantaged youth to sell useful products at affordable prices to people living in slums in Nairobi, thus having impact at both the individual and household levels. Joy wanted to really make an impact at the organization, so she used her personal networks to build a high-profile corporate partnership that would improve the lives of thousands of people by providing a significant discount. Sadly, the program failed; ultimately, the youth sales agents felt that the cheaper product didn't provide a big enough commission, and they refused to market it.

"This is the type of well-intentioned failure that is endemic to impact work. But it wasn't a total loss by any means. On the contrary, Joy learned—in a hands-on, unforgettable way—an invaluable lesson about the process of social change, one that she could never have gained through a $100,000 Ivy-League MBA. She now has a better understanding of what it takes to succeed and is more prepared to anticipate problems and overcome barriers in her path. This is why internships are so important. Even though they sometimes get a bad rap for being exploitative, they remain one of the best ways of gaining on-the-job learning experiences."

"But what if I'd rather create my own organization? I have some ideas to combat climate change," interrupted Kim.

Ilaina nodded. "You're reading our minds! That is our second-most-preferred option to acquire social impact skills—to **start your own project or organization**. By doing so, you will practice and master some of the most required skills in the sector. One of the key elements in our social innovation management post-graduate program is for the participants to conceive and develop a social innovation project. By starting something on your own, you practice an iterative process of creation and learn what it means to work toward a vision, how to fail and be resilient enough to start again, how to manage people, tasks, resources, and time, and how to build a support network for your idea and yourself.

"For example, Morris Litvak, an Amani Fellow from Brazil, created Maturi, the first organization that connects people older than fifty to opportunities for professional and personal development. Today, Maturi's online platform has registered more than 150,000 people from all states in Brazil and is becoming the country's go-to organization for older people to find employment. While building the organization, Morris learned how to build teams and partnerships and how to pivot when something is not working. He also learned how to be a great speaker and writer. Today, he is a lecturer and a columnist in a major Brazilian newspaper. He even learned how to organize events: in 2019 he ran the first festival catering to entrepreneurship and work for older professionals. The festival attracted more than five hundred people in just three days!"

Farah interjected. "Can I create a project inside an organization, rather than doing something on top of my full-time job?"

"Yes, that's certainly possible by being what's called a social intrapreneur, someone who promotes social change within established organizations," responded Ilaina. "Let me share another story to illustrate this. Shortly after achieving what he thought was his dream job at a well-known Indian food delivery service, Nikhil Goel was accepted into our social innovation management program in Kenya. Based on his food delivery expertise, he received an offer to work at a startup in Kenya that was looking to enter the food delivery market through its fleet of motorcycle riders. Most food delivery services in Nairobi typically focus on mainstream restaurants, leaving out the hundreds, if not thousands, of informal food vendors without a brick-and-mortar structure. Wanting to create social impact within the company, Nikhil began focusing on these informal food vendors, starting with the 'Mamas,' which are small woman-led food stands in Nairobi. He created a new project called Cha'kula to empower these small and informal food merchants across Nairobi, to increase their outreach, and thus their income."

"Another way to learn important skills is through what we are doing in this conversation, **learning from and with others**," said Roshan. "On June 7, 2012, at the launch party for our first office in Nairobi, we asked our guests to answer the question, 'What would your ideal education look like, if you could design it yourself?' One of our guests wrote: 'I would have more people guiding me through real-world wisdom and not just facts.' This speaks to a common theme among the thousands of people we have talked to about their higher education experience. There is a hunger to learn by observing other people's journeys—be it role models, mentors, or peers—as they provide a benchmark toward our desired future self. The American psychologist Daniel Levinson uses the term *guiding figures*—those who can help us to understand how to walk the path of a life of meaning and impact."[26]

"Tell us more about how to build a relationship with a role model or mentor," Kim pleaded.

"Sure!" said Ilaina. "First, think of someone who has achieved what you want to achieve, or has the characteristics and skills you admire. If you want a mentor and not just a role model, this person should be willing to share their wisdom with you. Then, because your role model or mentor is usually either already in your network or is known by someone who is, start by reaching out proactively within your network to find a way to get in touch with them. Finally, it is not just about finding the right person but about building a relationship with them. It's common to have role models whom we do not know personally but who can still help with inspiration and direction, such as Nelson Mandela or Oprah Winfrey. However, when learning new skills, it's better if we know them personally so we can watch how they deal with the ups and downs of their life. And, as with most relationships, we need to build it

---

26 Daniel J. Levinson, *The Seasons of a Woman's Life: A Fascinating Exploration of the Events, Thoughts, and Life Experiences That All Women Share*, (New York: Ballantine Books, 2011).

over time by being proactive and vulnerable, and expecting to give as well as to receive."

Farah looked thoughtful. "And what about my peers? I've learned a lot from my colleagues and friends as well."

"Absolutely," responded Roshan. "We don't learn from just those more experienced than us. Sometimes peers can share even deeper lessons than mentors because they face similar challenges in the present-day and not in the past."

Ilaina continued, "Finally, another creative way to learn important skills is by **immersing yourself into different contexts**. One way to do so is by traveling. Another Amani Fellow from Brazil, Gabriele Garcia, spent a year traveling with her husband through forty countries to witness social inequalities. They visited refugee camps, remote villages, NGOs, and social businesses in parts of Africa, the Middle East, and Asia. As Gabriele puts it, their primary motivation was 'to get out of the privileged bubble of two young white individuals,' and understand problems they had never experienced.

"But traveling does not have to mean visiting multiple countries, which of course can be quite expensive. The word 'safari' comes from Swahili and means *making a journey*. A safari could also be visiting the neighborhood next to yours but with a different perspective. Going to an unknown place allows you to step out of your comfort zone and can provide inspiration and time for reflection. We encourage you to go on many safaris!

We can even *safari* inside ourselves through meditation, which helps develop essential skills for social impact like creativity, empathy, focus, and self-awareness.[27] It provides opportunities for reflective learning, as we mentioned earlier."

"I know I've asked this question before, but I would love some ideas on how to immerse myself in different contexts," said Farah, her cat finally sleeping peacefully in her lap.

"Sure thing," said Roshan. "You must start with clarity about the *objectives of your journey*. When deciding what trip to take or even while meditating, reflect on what you want to gain from it. Do you need insights into a specific topic? Simply time to reflect? To understand how things happen in practice? Having clarity on your objectives will help you to better select or organize the right type of immersion experience. Second, it's important to both *prepare beforehand and take the time to reflect and savor afterward.* For example, should you research the people you are likely to meet? How will you introduce yourself to them? And when you return from the journey, spend some time harvesting your learning, like writing in a journal, for example. Finally, we

---

27 Danah Henriksen, Carmen Richardson, and Kyle Shack, "Mindfulness and Creativity: Implications for Thinking and Learning," *Thinking Skills and Creativity* 37, (September 2020), https://doi.org/10.1016/j.tsc.2020.100689; Viviana Capurso, Franco Fabbro, and Cristiano Crescentini, "Mindful Creativity: The Influence of Mindfulness Meditation on Creative Thinking," *Frontiers in Psychology* 4, (2014): 1020, https://doi.org/10.3389/fpsyg.2013.01020; J. Lutz, A. B. Brühl, H. Scheerer, L. Jäncke, and U. Herwig, "Neutral Correlates of Mindful Self-awareness in Mindfulness Mediators and Meditation-Naïve Subjects Revisited," *Biological Psychology* 119, (September 2016): 21–30, https://doi.org/10.1016/j.biopsycho.2016.06.010; Emory University, "Compassion Meditation May Boost Neural Basis of Empathy, Study Finds," Science Daily, October 4, 2012, https://www.sciencedaily.com/releases/2012/10/121004093504.htm. These studies explore the relationship between meditation and self-awareness, empathy, creativity, and focus.

suggest you *undertake as many journeys as possible*. You want to have as many experiences as you can to maximize your learning. Insights can come from anywhere!"

"I have a meeting starting soon," mentioned Ilaina. "Any final questions before we wrap up?"

TO DO OR NOT TO DO A MASTER'S DEGREE

"Yes!" said Kim. "With regard to designing our own education, you didn't say anything about educational training programs such as a master's degree. Though you mentioned that traditional universities aren't the right place to acquire social impact skills, I still have to ask...do you not recommend universities at all, or is there one in particular I should consider?"

"Rather than recommending a specific educational program," began Ilaina, "we've instead shared principles and methods that you can use to evaluate if an educational program is worth doing. While we believe in self-directing your own education, we also know of many excellent programs that have been created taking into account the principles described earlier."

Roshan continued, "About master's degrees specifically, the conventional wisdom is that there are three reasons to do one: knowledge, credentials, and networks. Let's take them one by one.

"First, master's degrees are more useful for acquiring knowledge than gaining professional skills. If you want an institution to curate and share cutting-edge research with you, then a master's makes sense. When you are an experienced practitioner, you can make the bridge from theory to practice on your own. But if you are just starting your career, you will most likely need to complement any master's degree with the other methods we've described. However, if you are less interested in knowledge for its own sake and want to build skills instead, you should avoid master's degrees because of their opportunity cost. In other words, how might you spend that time and money more effectively?

"That said, it's often still true that you need the credential of a master's degree because the type of job you want requires it. Although enlightened employers are increasingly moving away from requiring a master's degree, more bureaucratic and highly prestigious organizations still often use them as a way to filter out applicants in a highly competitive environment. The credential is thus valuable, but often not necessary if you can prove yourself on the job.

"Finally, many people choose a particular university or degree because they gain a network of people who share their interests and/or passions. Master's degree graduates often turn to their fellow alumni as a source of further opportunities and resources throughout their career. Thanks to the shared experience of the master's program, they are more emotionally invested in each other's success. However, master's degrees are certainly not the only way to find and join new networks these days. Many fellowship programs or local interest groups do the same thing. Finally, it's worth checking if the network the master's provides will be diverse enough. Remember that global problems cross all types of borders; you need a diverse network to make progress.

"As you can see, each of the three reasons for getting a master's degree are valid, but there are also counterarguments."

As we wrapped up the call, Kim and Farah repeatedly thanked us, but just as we were about to press the red "leave" button, Farah shyly asked, "The assignment you shared with us last time was so helpful. Might you have another assignment to keep us moving forward?"

We thought for a moment, and then Ilaina responded, "The next step is to identify what skills you need for the job you want. Of those skills, check off the ones you already have—and celebrate that! For the ones that you don't yet have, consider ways to get them, based on this conversation."

"Anything else we can do?" asked Kim.

"Why don't you visit our class next week?" Roshan offered. "We will be exploring crucial topics on personal alignment that will help you unlock your impact career aspirations. Deal?"

"Deal!" they said in unison.

ACTION AND REFLECTION

Act:

1. Identify three skills you still need to build your social impact career.

2. Using the learning principles and skill-acquisition methods described in this chapter, create a plan with at least three actionable items to acquire those skills.

3. Execute your plan.

Reflect:

1. How well did your formal education prepare you for an impact-first career? Which parts helped, and what was missing?

2. In your education, did you experience any of the learning principles or methods described in this chapter? In what ways did they help your learning?

4

ALIGNING WHO YOU ARE AND WHAT YOU DO

We were by the projector, putting last-minute touches on our session plan, when we saw Kim and Farah enter the classroom at Amani Institute. They came in hesitantly, as guests often do. Almost immediately, an Amani Fellow walked up and welcomed them, offered them a cup of coffee, and began introducing them to the other Fellows, a group of dynamic, highly motivated people from more than fifteen different countries. When we finally got to them, Kim and Farah commented how different the classroom was from what they had imagined: it had colorfully painted walls with Post-it Notes all over them, framed photographs of previous classes, beanbag chairs, easy laughter, and the smells of freshly baked bread and tropical fruit. They had already visibly relaxed.

THE INNER JOURNEY
OF THE CHANGEMAKER

Roshan kicked off the class. "Welcome to the Inner Journey of the Changemaker course. Based on our own careers and on working with thousands of changemakers around the world, we're certain this course will help you to sustain your impact for decades to come." The group was smiling with anticipation.

Ilaina continued, "Being a changemaker is not a traditional job, with fixed office hours or rewards measured in monetary terms. It connects to who you are, your values, and your mission in life. Understanding this is essential because social impact work tends to be deeply personal. Without caring personally about the problem, we simply wouldn't set out on this challenging and possibly transformational path. Furthermore, working toward impact is not only about what is visible: the job title, location, and the tasks you do; it's often just as much about the invisible things, what happens inside yourself."

Then Roshan pulled up a slide. "If we want to both responsibly and effectively bring change to the world, we need to develop the capacity to lead ourselves first, since how we relate to the world determines the impact we will have. The inner journey is, therefore, about the personal dimension of professional work in social change. It is reflective learning, curating a conversation with yourself while you act, as your values, purpose, and impact shift and grow over time. We must always be conscious of the interplay among our inner self, behaviors, and impact.

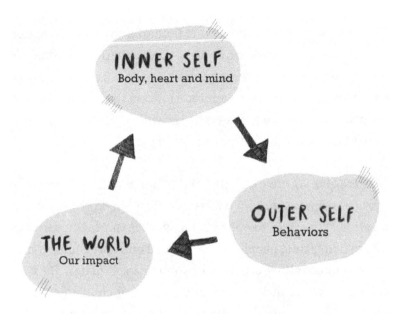

We use the word 'journey' because this process continues throughout your life as a social impact professional."

An Amani Fellow from the back of the class, a young youth leader from Perú, raised her hand: "So this is like self-awareness?"

Roshan nodded. "The inner journey starts with the oldest advice out there—'know thyself,' as the ancient Greeks exhorted us in the Temple of Apollo at Delphi. But that's just the beginning; next comes the journey toward becoming the best version of ourselves. Several of the world's most successful changemakers have confirmed that when we align with our deepest-held values and act from our inner wisdom, then we are more likely to unlock our potential to achieve greater impact for the world. However, 'knowing thyself' doesn't mean just focusing on inner work. It's not that you have to first change inside *before* creating change out in the world. Instead, the goal is deepening self-awareness while in action, through a continuous process of action and reflection."

"Let me give you an example," Ilaina jumped in. "When I was twenty-seven years old, I was sent to El Salvador by my organization at the time, to open up a new office there. Our mission was to help young people become social entrepreneurs, giving them opportunities other than joining local gangs. By that stage in my career, I had worked in several countries, had a master's degree, and had managed projects and people. But within twenty-four hours of landing in El Salvador, I realized I was not prepared for this. On the taxi from the airport, the driver commented that I'd just landed in a country with a homicide rate among the highest in the world. Things didn't improve when local leaders described how gangs were threatening their staff. And when, in a community meeting, looking to conserve our meager funds, I proposed that we use the same bus to pick up the different groups of young people that would participate in our program, I was told with rising alarm that this could lead to violence because youth from one gang would have to ride the bus through neighborhoods dominated by the other gang. To be successful in this job, what I needed was not a fancy degree or technical skills, but rather empathy, resilience, courage, hope, and so on. These qualities are all linked to my inner self: who I was and who I wanted to become. The year I spent doing that job was one of the best experiences in my life.

"I learned all those skills *while in action,* which is how you understand who you really are. American educator and activist Parker Palmer talks about being aware of one's own lights and shadows.[28] Your lights are your strengths, and recent research demonstrates how using their strengths helps changemakers be more productive, better leaders, more committed to their causes and, therefore, happier.[29] But it's important to also be aware of the darkness, as your shadows get projected onto other people. Palmer suggests that if you don't understand that the enemy is inside, you'll find countless ways to turn someone 'out there' into an enemy, which can turn you into someone who oppresses rather than liberates. Being self-aware means understanding your emotions, triggers, and limiting beliefs, as well as your strengths, desires, dreams, and visions."

Roshan then added, "One of the dangers of the self-awareness mantra, at least when applied to social impact, is a false 'doing versus being' dichotomy, which mistakenly conflates *doing* with the modern disease of *being busy.* We are often encouraged to move away from *doing* and focus more on *being.* This is sometimes used as an excuse to avoid getting into action. But being without doing is inadequate—only action can improve our world. Being and doing are infused in one movement, like breathing in and breathing out."

---

28 See *Let Your Life Speak,* by Parker Palmer.

29 Marcus Buckingham, *StandOut: The Groundbreaking New Strengths Assessment from the Leader of the Strengths Revolution (Nashville: Thomas Nelson Inc., 2011);* Tom Rath, *StrengthsFinder 2.0* (Washington, DC: Gallup, 2007); "Live Your Best Life Using Your Strengths," Gallup, access date July 13, 2021, https://www.gallup.com/cliftonstrengths/en/252137/home.aspx.

You could feel the words beginning to take effect in the group. There was a deep, reflective silence. The words were still sinking in when Farah raised her hand and asked: "This all makes sense, but where do we start?"

PLANTING SEEDS: YOUR SIGNS OF AWAKENING

"Good question!" Roshan exclaimed. "The first step is asking why, truly, we want to be changemakers. For some, motivation comes from a single transformative moment, what we call a sign of awakening. For others, it's a slow burn, a growing conviction that changemaking is necessary to live a fulfilling life. Understanding what initially fueled your motivation serves both as a compass *and* a source of renewal during your life as a changemaker. It becomes your north star, keeping you going forward when everything seems dark.

"To start exploring our motives for being a changemaker, let's try an exercise called *collecting your signs of awakening*. We define a sign of awakening as a specific time when we suddenly became aware of something larger than ourselves that angered, saddened, inspired, or delighted us, making us want to act in some way to improve the human condition."

"Can you give us an example?" asked Kim.

"Sure," said Ilaina. "I was twelve years old when I saw a Pulitzer Prize-winning photograph taken at Trang Bàng during the

Vietnam War by photographer Nick Ut. The picture shows soldiers and civilians running after an airplane napalm attack. It vividly depicts the horrors of the war, but what caught my attention was a girl who might have been about the same age as me. I was comfortably reading a book while this girl was fleeing in terror, naked and full of despair. If our places were reversed, what would I have hoped the girl reading the book would do?"

Roshan continued, "I've previously shared my own sign of awakening on 9/11. As you can see, a sign of awakening could come from a major global event, from reading something in a book, watching a movie, or even just observing how your parents behaved when you were little."

"Now, it's time for you to reflect on your own signs of awakening," Ilaina continued. "Find those moments that motivated you to be where you are today, pursuing a career of meaning and impact. Here are some questions to prompt your thinking: When have you witnessed injustice? Have you ever watched a documentary or read a book that transformed you? Have you ever met someone who changed the way you thought about something? Have you taken a trip that changed how you see the world? Have you ever been the 'other' or in the minority? Is there anything in your family's story (grandparents, parents, yourself) that inspires you to be a changemaker?"

The room was utterly silent. Some looked to the floor or ceiling for inspiration, others closed their eyes, still others walked to the window and stared out. We started to hear birdsong in the trees outside and traffic in the distance. After roughly twenty minutes, some of the group started moving to the coffee station. They had finished the exercise—and it was clearly time for a break!

During the break, Farah and Kim approached us. Ilaina asked them, "Any insights from the exercise so far?"

"Yes!" said Farah, smiling widely. "I discovered a common thread that connects all my signs of awakening. The role of women in society. I had an inkling when I got so triggered by my company promoting a woman at a lower salary than her male counterpart. Yet, at the time, I didn't know I had so many other signs of awakening connected to this issue too."

Kim frowned. "I was expecting to see signs of awakening connected to climate change because that is the issue I want to work on. But I didn't find the connections."

"All good observations," Ilaina responded. "We will explore these insights more after the break. Let me grab a coffee before we start!"

FINDING DIRECTION: UNCOVERING YOUR PURPOSE

When everyone had taken their seats, Roshan, still holding his steaming cup of coffee, asked the group what they learned from listing signs of awakening. Everyone took turns sharing. One person remarked, "At the beginning, it was hard to identify the signs, but then they started to flow like water." Several heads nodded emphatically in agreement.

Then Roshan continued, "Signs of awakening help us understand our intrinsic motivation. For instance,"—and here Roshan winked at Kim—"climate change may be a manifestation of the deeper problem you really care about, like stewardship of the planet, a desire to not spoil it for future generations, a simple love for natural beauty, and so on. All of these are harmed by climate change. So, it's not climate change *per se* that matters, but deeper values that are at stake as the world gets hotter, more inhospitable, and dangerous. Ultimately, we realize our children's lives will be less pleasant than our own.

"So, you need to dig more deeply for clarity of purpose—why are you choosing to act now? Stanford professor William Damon describes purpose as 'a stable and generalized intention to accomplish something that is at the same time meaningful to the self and consequential for the world beyond the self.'"[30]

Ilaina continued, "Some people's purpose might be deeply connected with a specific topic like *end poverty* or *educate children*. Others may care more about fostering a set of values or a vision like *a world where everyone is free to be themselves* or *a more loving world*. The importance of a life purpose is that it provides direction for your career and helps you stay on track during difficult times. As we have discussed previously, an increasing number of people are hungry to build careers

---

30 William Damon, *The Path to Purpose: Helping Our Children Find Their Calling in Life*, (New York: Free Press, 2008).

where there is a larger purpose than making money. We also talked about how a sense of purpose is a crucial predictor of job satisfaction. Therefore, when looking for an impact-first job, ask yourself: which jobs will help me achieve my purpose?"

Another Amani Fellow, a vivacious young digital media professional from Nigeria, raised her hand. "So is your purpose what you do, or is it more like who you are?"

"It could be either," replied Roshan, "depending on how you frame it. One of our mentors, Rajiv Ball, who helped design the approach to leadership development at McKinsey & Company but now helps lead THNK, an organization dedicated to fostering creative leaders, says that his purpose, when framed as what he does, is to 'help leaders grow, so that they can positively affect the world.' But Rajiv also frames his purpose as who he is, and in this framing, he is 'a gentle Sherpa who helps leaders realize their potential to impact their world.' Here, Rajiv is using the imagery and symbolism of a *Sherpa*, who helps mountain climbers in Nepal, to show how he wants to help leaders 'climb the mountain of making impact,' so to speak.

"As you can see, it's really up to you. So how would you define your purpose? Please take a few minutes to think about framing your purpose as something you do, or a *doing* statement, as well as framing it as part of who you are, a *being* statement."

Ilaina turned on some soft background music, and the class scattered to various corners to ruminate on their life purpose. When we reconvened, another Amani Fellow, a former investment banker from China, raised his hand. "Let's say that my purpose is crystal clear. Now how do I find a job? It's a big leap from clarifying my purpose to making it happen in the real world."

OVERCOMING OBSTACLES: HOW YOUR BELIEFS HOLD YOU BACK OR DRIVE YOU FORWARD

"Great question!" exclaimed Ilaina. "Often, the biggest thing holding us back from pursuing our purpose is the beliefs we have about ourselves, others, and the world."

"What exactly do you mean by beliefs here?" asked the Fellow who had raised his hand.

Ilaina's eyes twinkled. "When I was four years old, I overheard my mother and sister discussing my sister's boyfriend. With a big, world-weary sigh, I commented, 'All men are the same, Mom.' My mother was stunned. She said, 'Ilaina, I don't believe you just said that. Where did you get it from?' I couldn't confess this to her, but I had heard it in a soap opera that my sister and I watched secretly when my parents were at work. If my mother had not confronted this cynical belief, I may well have grown up and made decisions based on the belief that all men are the same, not realizing it was from a soap opera I would never watch today!"

Everyone laughed out loud. Ilaina continued, "We are not born with our beliefs. We develop them through our lives, adopting them from our family, classmates, and societal culture. Our basic assumptions are often hidden from our conscious awareness. We might think we know ourselves when we don't. We believe we're making choices from free will, but we're actually conditioned by prior beliefs. If we're aware of and can challenge our own beliefs, we can gain more freedom than we imagine."

Farah burst in, "Are you saying I might not pursue an impact-first career because my preconceived beliefs stop me from doing so?"

"Exactly!" confirmed Ilaina. "Self-limiting beliefs are extremely common. For example, regarding skills, we've heard people say, 'I don't have the skills to raise money for my cause.' In other cases, self-limiting beliefs are about one's stage in life: 'I'm too old to chase a new career dream.' Beliefs can also come from uncertainty or fear: 'What if I fail?'"

Most Fellows were nodding their heads in agreement. Two of them asked, simultaneously, "But what can we do about this?"

"Once you encounter a self-limiting belief, start by challenging it until you move into an *empowering belief*. I need a volunteer!" invited Ilaina.

"Me!" said Farah.

"Great," said Ilaina. "Please share a limiting belief about pursuing an impact-first career."

Farah thought for a few moments and then slowly said, "I will never find a job in social impact because I have no experience in the sector."

Ilaina nodded. "The first step is to ask yourself if this is actually true. Farah, is it really true that you will *never* find a job in social impact because you have never worked in the sector?"

Farah smiled and said, "Ok, maybe I shouldn't say *never*. If I do some internships or consulting for impact-first organizations, I can start building some experience."

"Well done!" cheered Ilaina. "The next step is to convert your self-limiting belief into an empowering one."

Another Fellow, a social entrepreneur from Egypt, raised her hand. "Can you please clarify what you mean by a self-limiting belief and empowering one?"

"Sure," said Ilaina. "Self-limiting beliefs are ideas and assumptions that stop us from achieving our goals. On the other hand, empowering beliefs enable us to flourish. Most beliefs aren't intrinsically self-limiting or empowering; it's us who make them so. Thus, we can change them; we can edit them! When we were thinking about opening our first Amani Institute office, one option was Nairobi, Kenya. We were excited by that. It meant walking our talk, stepping out of our comfort zone, and being bold. Those beliefs helped us to be proud of our courage, and thus more willing to confront all the challenges that come with starting a new organization in a foreign country.

"By contrast, we could just as easily have believed that opening our first office in a country we had spent very little time in, where we didn't know many people or even the culture, was doomed to fail. If we'd believed that, you wouldn't be in this classroom today. Your belief about starting something new in an unknown place—whether exciting or foolish—comes from your own experiences, your past, and the influence of family, friends, and culture. My parents have repeatedly started a new life in different countries, so for me it was always possible. Roshan's dad started a management consulting firm in the 1970s when India was still a socialist country without much of a private sector. And we've both worked with hundreds of social entrepreneurs who have started new organizations against huge odds. All these influences shaped our belief that this choice of Nairobi would be doable.

"And while it is important to know where your beliefs are coming from, it is even more important to understand if they serve you in the present, or not. Do your beliefs help you pursue your dreams?"

"So, Farah, can you reframe your belief to be empowering?" asked Roshan.

After reflecting a bit, Farah responded proudly, "I have transferable skills that will allow me to gain entry into impact-first jobs. And I am determined to convince people to give me a chance to show my potential." The class broke into applause.

Roshan continued, "Awareness of your beliefs is critical, because choosing an impact-first career is still not a conventional choice in much of the world. It is easier to claim that you want to be a doctor, engineer, lawyer, or coder. It's much harder to explain why you want to become a changemaker. Let's go around the room: how many of your family members really understand what you want from your career?"

Most of the group shook their heads ruefully, having tried, often unsuccessfully, to explain their life choices to their loved ones.

Roshan continued, "Shortly after I returned to India after graduating college in the US, I attended a friend's wedding reception. Now, a favorite topic of the older generation is matchmaking young people with each other. At the reception, I found myself in a conversation with a woman of my mother's generation. She said, with a big smile, 'I heard you're based in America.' Here we go, I thought. 'No, I returned to India after graduating,' I said.

"Her smile dimmed a little. 'Oh, but you must be working for a consulting firm or an IT company, right?'

"'No, I work in an NGO', I said.

"Her smile vanished and she edged away to talk to someone else. At that moment, I knew my stock in the Indian marriage market had officially plummeted to the bottom!"

As the laughter died down, Roshan added, "If you've grown up hearing that the social sector is for bored housewives or volunteers or is 'not a real job,' then you aren't alone. I grew up hearing the same things. But do we want those beliefs to define our future?"

STANDING YOUR GROUND: GIVING VOICE TO VALUES

At the back of the room, we could see a new conversation had broken out between Farah and Kim. Ilaina invited them to share.

"My parents don't support my desire to pursue an impact-first career," Kim confessed. He looked sad. "I don't want their opinions to define my life; and yet I'm also uncomfortable to go against their wishes. We just have different values!"

Ilaina nodded. "Even once we've chosen the beliefs that will shape our careers, we must remember that we are not islands. Our decisions might clash with the values of people we love or the society we belong to.

"We've all faced situations where we know what the right thing to do is, but because it's hard or risky to act accordingly, we end up going against what we believe is right. One person who observed this phenomenon, particularly among MBA students who go on to lead companies and thus face ethical decisions all the time, is Dr. Mary Gentile, a professor at the University of Virginia. After studying this gap between people's values and their actions, she developed a curriculum called Giving Voice to Values (GVV).

"GVV is a method to help you put your values into practice. The framework assumes that most of us want to act in line with our values but also want to feel we have a reasonable chance of doing so effectively. Therefore, before confronting a situation where values are in conflict, it's worth preparing for the conversation. There are three tips to consider.

"*First, seek common ground.* We often believe our values should be embraced by everyone, but as we know, especially in today's era of polarization and filter bubbles, major differences in people's values may never be reconciled, because those values are shaped by vastly different cultural, political, and religious backgrounds. If we look closely, however, we can also find common values across diverse contexts and cultures. So, consider which values are important for both you and the person you are talking with. Then, e*ngage in a purpose-driven conversation.* When we start a conversation grounded in purpose, there is a greater chance that the other person also engages in a deeper conversation. Finally, *find your voice.* When voicing your values, don't preach, but rather engage in a dialogue where both parties listen and ask questions. While strong emotions tend to emerge in these types of conversations, we can work hard to manage our own emotions as well as do our best not to push the other's buttons and trigger resentment and resistance."[31]

---

31 Mary Gentile, "Ethical Leadership Through Giving Voice to Values," online course, University of Virginia, https://www.coursera.org/learn/uva-darden-giving-voice-to-values/home/week/2.

"And what if I'm still not able to convince my parents?" asked Kim.

Ilaina responded, "You can still decide whether to act on your own values or follow theirs. You are free to make and accept the consequences of your decision, whether your parents don't talk to you because of your career choice or whether you don't pursue your dreams because you prioritize family harmony. In either case, it's *you* who decides based on what your true values are. However, if we prepare well for the conversation, we can usually find common ground."

ALIGNMENT: WALKING THE TIGHTROPE

Roshan switched to another topic, mindful of the clock ticking. "The process of monitoring your alignment with these concepts—your signs of awakening, purpose, core values—and realigning when needed is the core of the inner journey of the changemaker. Another of our advisors, Jerry White—who was a recognized leader of International Campaign to Ban Landmines, which won the Nobel Peace Prize in 1997—has always exhorted us to be mindful of living an aligned, and not fragmented, life. As Jerry puts it, 'Transformational leaders align three things: I call them Wisdom, Understanding, and Knowledge. Call them whatever you like, whether Value-set, Mindset, and Skillset; or Awareness, Advocacy, and Action; even Mind-Body-Spirit. Just make sure these three essential layers align *who* you are, *why* you seek change, and *what* you do...day to day.'[32]

---

32 "Spotlight: Jerry White," Business Impact, accessed July 13, 2021, https://businessimpact.umich.edu/jerry-white/.

"Thus, you live an aligned life when those three aspects are integrated in a way that moves you toward your purpose and doesn't cause inner conflicts. It's like walking a tightrope. In pursuit of your goals, fortified by the motivation coming from your signs of awakening, when the going gets tough and you realize that you are about to fall, you have to return to the center. And what brings you back to your center is your purpose and your values."

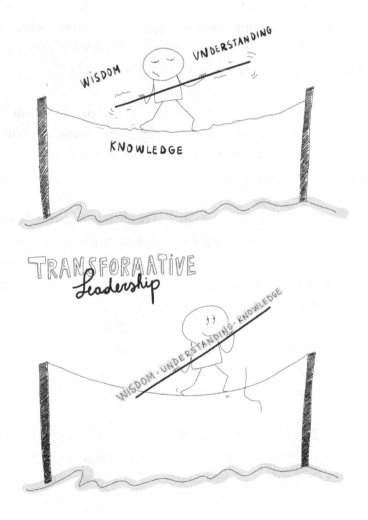

YOU WILL BE CALLED TO SHOW COURAGE

Roshan continued, "We know that walking the alignment tightrope is easier said than done. It requires courage. Let's end with a story of how we ourselves were called upon to show courage and alignment and give voice to our values.

"One morning in May 2014 in Nairobi, we were awakened at 7:00 a.m. by our office assistant. Amani Institute was just two years old at the time. She called to say, 'I can't get in to clean the office. There's a police action on your building.'

"That sounded bizarre. We had no idea what she meant. We went on Twitter and started to glean that there had been a burglary attempt and the police were engaged in an armed standoff with the burglars.

"In about two hours, our cohort of twenty-two Amani Fellows was due to show up for a full day of class. We had to swing into action right away. We phoned a co-working space we knew and booked their conference room for a day. We then sent a message on our WhatsApp group: 'Don't go to the office under any circumstances. Class is shifted to Nairobi Garage. Please go there.' We followed that message with individual calls to make sure everyone knew not to go to the office. And with just a short delay, we were underway in class as usual."

Ilaina jumped in. "It's important to know the context of May 2014 in Nairobi. Between April and June, bombs and terrorist attacks took place in bus stations, crowded markets, and so on.

This was largely carried out by terrorist groups from Somalia in retaliation for Kenya's military presence in their country. The atmosphere in Nairobi was tense, and a number of organizations, such as the US Peace Corps and large church groups, decided to leave the country. There were travel warnings not to come to Kenya, and one of our friends said he couldn't attend a close friend's wedding because he would lose his job if his organization found out. Not the best timing to run a global education program!

"Going back to that day, we got a call from the building management a few hours later. 'The coast is clear and it's safe to come back,' they promised us.

"One of our team members decided to go back to our office building to retrieve some valuables because, in these situations, an attack is often followed by looting. About an hour later, we got a panicked call from him, telling us he was now stuck in the office because the police had discovered more burglars hiding in the building and were yelling that everyone should stay behind locked doors. These burglars were all heavily armed, by the way."

Roshan picked up the thread. "And just like that, one of our employees was in the vicinity of a gunfight. I left the co-working space and rushed over to our office, about ten minutes away. A few people had gathered outside, friends and family members of others who had gone into the building and were now stuck as well. Everyone around me was nervous and scared. The police began yelling at us to hide behind the building wall so that if bullets started to fly, we wouldn't get caught in the cross-fire. And so I was hiding behind the wall of my office building, thinking about my colleague, whose life was in danger.

"A few minutes later, it was over. The police overcame the burglars and our colleague emerged from the building, emotionally shaken but unharmed.

"That night, we had to process what had happened. Though this attack had nothing to do with terrorism—it was an armed robbery on a rich company in the same building—it still felt different. This wasn't a mall or a bus stop or a market, all of which we were avoiding in those days. This time it had hit our office, where we spent every day. It felt personal. We had to decide what we were going to do.

"We held an emergency meeting that night with some of our advisors. We met in a dark wine bar. And we had to decide: should we stay or should we go? We were facing a lot of pressure, even before this incident happened, from parents of our students, our board members, and some of our partners. They were all asking: Is Kenya safe? Should we be there at all?

"We talked about it for a long time, until the bar closed; the staff went home and left us there, weighing pros and cons late into the night."

The whole classroom was leaning forward in their chairs. Not a sound could be heard as Ilaina continued.

"In the end, we decided to stay. After all, the reason we came to Kenya, the reason we didn't set up in New York or Amsterdam or Singapore, was because there's this dynamic of complicated problems, on the one hand, but also possibility and rapid progress on the other hand. We truly believe that the future is being written in emerging markets and, as an organization working in social innovation, it's important to be in an innovative place, to be on the frontlines. And Nairobi is one of the most innovative cities on the planet, having led in the development of things like crowd-mapping and mobile money, which have now spread globally. It is a city that has changed the world.

"So, we decided not to close shop. But we also decided that if anyone didn't feel safe anymore, because safety has to be a personal decision for each individual, then we wouldn't stop them from leaving. We would even refund their fees.

"But, and here's where alignment with our values comes in, we wouldn't let them graduate if they left. *Being there* was part of their learning how to be a changemaker.

"And that led to problems for us. Our university partner at the time, which in those early days was very important to our credibility, decided to end the partnership. We lost a number of tuition-paying students because of that. We eventually canceled a whole program. And one of our Fellows from that class was so angry that we wouldn't let her do the rest of the program online that she still doesn't talk to us to this day! So we endured some painful losses because we made a decision in line with our values."

Roshan chimed in. "However, apart from that one student who wanted to leave, the other twenty-one had no doubts about staying and continuing with the program. We were so proud of our Fellows; their courage and commitment were two of the main reasons we knew we had made the right decision. We put our heads down and went back to work. The next eighteen months or so were tough, and we often wondered if we would survive, but then the tide started to turn. We won a contract to train hundreds of young African leaders each year, and we expanded to Brazil and then to India. The organization became financially sustainable. We also got invited to give a TED Talk and speak at the White House and began to win education awards. Things were better than ever before.

"But none of that would have happened if we had left Kenya in May 2014. So that 7:00 a.m. phone call from our office assistant was a wake-up call to stand for our values and do the things we believe in.

"As we said earlier, changing the world requires courage—the courage to retain our idealism in a cynical world, to remain true to ourselves in a career that requires tough choices and trade-offs as much in our personal lives (relationships, family, money) as in our workplaces and the communities we seek to serve; the courage to recognize what and how we can do better; the courage to step outside our comfort zones and stretch into new possibilities; the courage to manage our fears and those of our colleagues throughout the journey of changemaking; the courage to give and invite feedback from others about how we can collectively improve, to be open and vulnerable while building relationships. And in leadership, it may also require the courage to say no to corruption or to end a beloved program that is no longer working, or even to face physical threats from those who do not want the world to change. We wish you this courage, to align who you are and what you do as you build your own impact-first career of meaning and impact."

With that, the session closed. There was a distinct buzz as everyone began to gather their things and make evening plans.

Kim and Farah approached us. "Thanks for inviting us today," said Farah. "It's the kind of real talk we would never get in a university program. And, of course, it's so valuable even for those of us well into our careers to keep reflecting on all of this."

"What are you doing this weekend?" Kim asked impulsively. "Would you like to go on a hike together? I'm sure we'll have many more questions by then!"

We laughed. "Sure, let's meet at the park on Saturday," Roshan said. "A hike will probably do us good."

ACTION AND REFLECTION

Act:

1. Identify ten signs of awakening and look for common threads among them.

2. Write down your purpose (framed either as a "doing" or "being" statement).

3. Identify five empowering beliefs that encourage you to pursue an impact-first career. Then identify five that are limiting you from pursuing one—and try and reframe them into empowering beliefs.

Reflect:

1. Are there specific people with whom you might need to "give voice to your values"?

2. What does alignment look like for you?

5

BECOMING A SOCIAL
INNOVATOR

Saturday morning dawned bright and clear, a few scattered clouds dotting a breezeless sky. It was clearly going to be a hot summer day.

"Cute dog!" Farah exclaimed at the park gates, squatting down to pet Ilaina's golden retriever, Punky, who had come along for the walk. Punky pretended to bite her ear playfully in response.

"Looks like you're getting ready to have your ear chewed off in more ways than one," Roshan remarked dryly.

Farah chuckled and straightened up. "I can't wait. Shall we go in?"

We walked through the park gates and chose a winding path strewn with flowers discarded by huge, old trees on either side, their canopies providing a welcome shade from the summer heat. As we settled into our stride, Kim started, "I must confess that I feel a bit down today. Encouraged by our online meeting, I decided to start a new project to tackle climate change."

Farah whistled. "Kim, you're going to become an entrepreneur!"

Kim blushed. "Not so fast...I was just doing it to acquire social impact skills and understand the climate change problem better. Designing my own education! As recommended, I also decided to share it with some of my college friends. However, all I received was destructive feedback. By the end of that meeting, I was in despair, feeling I was doing everything wrong."

TEARING DOWN IS EASIER THAN BUILDING UP

"I am sorry to hear that, Kim, but I'm not surprised," said Ilaina, bending down to retrieve a large flower that Punky was gleefully ripping to shreds. "It is far easier to tear something down than to build a new alternative in the first place. We've learned throughout history that it's simpler to start a revolution against the existing system than to reform that system once you're in power. The same dynamic takes place every day in workplaces; what frustrates employers more than anything else is when a staff member points out something that is going wrong but doesn't have any ideas to fix it. Essentially, they are putting the onus of problem-solving higher up the food chain. Sometimes this is appropriate. But nothing builds your employer's trust and confidence more than if you also share some possible solutions to address that problem. It's even more frustrating when the staffer looks pleased with themselves for having presented their critique, as if their job is done. And yet perhaps it's unfair to blame them because this is all they were taught to do."

"And therein lies the failure of higher education," Roshan added. "As we mentioned in our online meeting, since the province of higher education is research, analysis, and critical thinking, graduates leave university believing those skills are all they need in the real world."

"Surely that's not always the case," Kim objected. "Aren't there some fields of study out there that get it right?"

"Of course," Roshan admitted. "Medicine for example. Or the military. When the stakes are, literally, life and death, we get it right because we must. A surgeon who has never done surgery won't get many patients, a soldier who has never fired a weapon won't be sent out in combat. And yet, we routinely graduate 'masters' in international development or business administration or name-your-generic-master's-degree who have never seen a program or a business get set up and succeed or fail in the real world. Sometimes a master's graduate in international development has never even left their home country; frequently, a master's graduate in conflict resolution has never been to an actual conflict zone," Roshan finished, panting a little as the path steepened and the cobblestones gave way to mud.

Punky raced ahead, scornfully glancing back at the humans moving at a glacially slow pace as far as she was concerned. Farah adjusted the backpack she was carrying and braced herself for the climb. As we started uphill, Roshan continued, "If there's one skill you need to master for social impact, that your university almost certainly didn't help you learn, it's the skill of problem-solving in the real world. How do you fix something that's broken? How do you generate a new idea when all immediate solutions have been found wanting? Can you build something new from the debris of the past? When you see a flaw in someone's thinking, how can you not only point it out but show a better way forward?

"This skill will become ever more important in the years to come. Even before the COVID-19 pandemic, nearly all employers agreed that the world (and the operating environment for organizations) was changing faster and faster, and they could barely keep up. When nobody has a clue what the world is going to look like in five, ten, or fifteen years, how can we educate ourselves and others for that world? Perhaps we can't. But there are a handful of skills that will always be useful, skills like resilience, adaptability, and empathy. And, problem-solving."

INNOVATION-THE SUPER SKILL WE CAN ALL POSSESS

We had reached the top of the hill, the woody hillsides giving way to a large grassy meadow. We paused to catch our breath as Punky bounded back toward us, joyful at having acres of space to run around in. Ilaina pulled out a small ball and threw it for her to chase.

"What makes someone good at problem-solving?" Kim asked.

"Innovation," Roshan said. "The ability to find new and better ways of doing things."

"Isn't that something you're just born with and thus some have an advantage over others?" asked Farah.

"Whether or not that's true," Ilaina replied, "it's also true that innovation can be learned. It can be *practiced*, and it can be deliberately *applied*."

"So how do you help people learn innovation at Amani Institute?" Kim challenged.

The grass was so soft that we all took off our shoes to feel the pleasure of walking barefoot. "At Amani Institute, the skill of innovation is the red thread or the foundational skill upon which most of our programs are built," said Ilaina. "We even designed a framework for it—the Amani Social Innovation

Framework. We built it by drawing from the study of innovation in the high-tech sector, utilizing methodologies made popular by the Design Thinking approach to problem-solving, and adding best practices from social entrepreneurship. The framework guides participants through the process of generating and testing ideas to solve a problem that they care about, be it a new product, process or service, and whether inside or outside an organization."

"In fact, all our Fellows, the ones you met in class the other day, learn and apply this framework," Roshan added. "We show them how to apply structure to the process of innovation. So far, more than 540 people from sixty-five countries have developed ideas for problems they care about solving. We've also helped major impact-first organizations like UNICEF and Oxfam do this for their own teams or beneficiaries. And every now and then, an Amani Fellow becomes so captivated with their idea that they turn it into an actual social venture after they graduate."

"I want to hear the story of one such project," said Farah. "But first, I have a surprise!"

She put down her backpack and began to remove several items from it, starting with a series of Tupperware boxes and a large sarong. "I made a picnic for us," she smiled. "Anyone hungry?"

"Amazing!" the rest of us exclaimed. We spread out the sarong and sat down.

"Tell us about one of these Fellows and how they applied the framework you mentioned," said Farah, as she began laying out the picnic.

"One such example comes from Gianmarco Marinello, who goes by Gian," Roshan began. "Gian is a tall and lanky Swiss who was a financial analyst prior to attending Amani Institute. He'd had an inkling for a while that he was meant to make a difference in the world. As he went from job to job in his twenties, he found himself searching for the traditional wise mentor to tell him what he was good at and what to do. He never found that person, but he realized he was in fact playing this role for others. He traveled to South Africa to volunteer in a township, and that's where he discovered his purpose: to help disadvantaged youth discover their full potential. He came to Amani Institute to learn how to do that better.

"Along with his classmate Sriram Damodaran, a former technology professional from India, Gian developed an idea for a social enterprise called Nai Nami, which means 'Nairobi with me' in Sheng, the street language of Nairobi. Nai Nami provides storytelling tours in the city center of Nairobi led by former street children, which allows tourists to experience Nairobi through the eyes and life stories of a street child. By leading these tours, these young people get meaningful work that allows them to transcend their background and become modern professionals, with the hope of lifting them out of poverty and into middle-class lives. As of 2020, the Nai Nami guides had hosted four thousand visitors to Nairobi from over one hundred countries. Their tour has been rated the number one Nairobi experience on TripAdvisor. More importantly, these guides have become role models for their communities, and some of them have moved out of the slum and into apartment buildings. In 2019, Gian and Sriram handed the organization over to the youth to lead it. Sriram has dedicated his professional future to wildlife conservation. Gian, now back in Switzerland, is still involved as business developer and advisor of Nai Nami, while also consulting to several different organizations as he works out his next big step."

Kim whistled. "That's an amazing—and somewhat intimidating—story," he said.

Ilaina was quick to reassure him. "But it wasn't an easy or straightforward journey. By developing their idea through the Amani Social Innovation Framework, Gian and Sriram intentionally applied the skills and behaviors of innovation toward addressing the problem of youth unemployment and disenfranchisement in Nairobi. Our point is that this is something anyone can do!"

HOW TO BECOME AN INNOVATOR

"But how?" Kim cried out. "I tried to build my climate change project, but it still needs so much work!"

Ilaina nodded. "In our experience, innovation hangs on a set of six underlying skills and behaviors that can be applied by anybody to solve problems.

⋛ LEARN how to be INNOVATIVE ⋚

ASKiNG MoRE QuESTioNS

Living the problem

REFRAMiNG

associAting

finding the FLiP

DOiNG is The best way of THINKING

"First, it's critical to develop a practice of **asking more questions** than those around you. We've been educated so thoroughly toward finding the right answer within a specified period of time that our conditioned instinct is to move as fast as possible in the direction of an answer—any answer that will pass muster. And yet one of the most powerful skills is learning how to ask the right questions. Before we step into problem-solving, we first need to engage in problem *finding*.

"Problems are tricky things; they hide as much as they reveal, and it's often not clear on the surface just what the problem is. If you see a child playing on the street in Mumbai, is that because her parents can't afford to send her to school? Or because there is no school where she lives? Or because the school is so awful she may as well not be there? Or because she gets bullied in school? Or because there are no toilets in her school and she is nearing puberty? Or is she simply playing hooky from school?

"Even if we take just one of those scenarios—let's say her parents cannot afford to send her to school—there's a new set of questions to consider. Is that because they are unemployed? Or are they too deeply in debt? Or because her father drinks away all his income? Each of these questions points to a different root cause, and therefore a different solution. We can ask several more such questions for each possible reason she isn't in school. This is vital because the first solution that perhaps comes to mind—for example, let's give her a scholarship so her parents can afford school—quite possibly will not solve the problem. The difficulty of getting to the root cause of the problem is one reason why social problems are so devilishly difficult to solve. And when you factor in not just one root of the problem but multiple root causes, and now you're really in the thick of it!"

"Those who come up with creative new solutions are usually good at resisting the urge to jump to the first solution that comes to mind," Roshan added. "This would be a good time to quote Einstein's famous and perhaps apocryphal line—that if he had an hour to solve a problem, he would spend the first fifty-five minutes asking the right questions. But Einstein today is a legend on the way to achieving mythical status—and therefore easy to ignore. So, let's go back to our mid-thirties Swiss man seeking to contribute to the world.

"When Gian recently spoke to us about Nai Nami's progress, his eyes gleamed as he said, 'People often ask if I'm a journalist or a spy, because I ask so many questions! If you can ask why, why, why, with the mindset of a three-year-old, and ask people who are not normally asked for their opinion, then you start to understand the problem in all its dimensions. Anyone can do this—it takes no special skills. Yet, most people don't do it. So, if you do it, you gain an advantage in understanding what's really going on.'

"Gian is right that it takes no special skills. What it does take is *unlearning* the rush to find the right answer. Creative people are able to keep their instinctive answers and assumptions at bay, to take a second, third, and fourth look, to ask different questions to different people involved in the issue, and even, in some cases, to follow the advice of Austrian poet Rainer Maria Rilke, who urged us to live the questions, until one day you live your way into the answer."

"Let's move to the second behavior that's critical for innovation," said Ilaina. "We know that solutions rarely come from that mythical lightbulb moment or epiphany. One of the key parts of the Amani Social Innovation Framework is what we call *sensing*, which is **immersing yourself into the problem** even when you are not directly affected by it. The college students who lived in Guatemala for four months on one dollar a day[33] are better positioned to understand poverty than if they had only studied poverty at a university and never actually experienced it in the real world, which is the case of many students of international development. If you want to solve a problem, try and experience it yourself if possible. When we first ran a course in Brazil, some of our students wanted to improve working conditions for pregnant women. They designed a fake stomach that weighed six kilograms and took turns wearing it for a day to understand some aspects of what it means to work while pregnant. Another group spent a significant amount of time with homeless people in the streets to understand how they saw the world.

"But if being in someone else's shoes is impossible, we need to spend quality time having conversations with those affected by the problem. I once visited a small town at the foot of Mount Imbabura, a volcano in Ecuador, to check out the work of an

---

33 "Living on One Dollar," Wikimedia Foundation, last modified April 8, 2021, 18:54, https://en.wikipedia.org/wiki/Living_on_One_Dollar.

international NGO. With the best of intentions, that organization had built outdoor toilets for the indigenous community, who previously had no choice but to defecate or urinate in the open, which of course has a number of negative consequences for both health and safety. When I arrived, those brand-new toilets had been turned into storage rooms, nursery gardens, or simply dismantled and repurposed for 'more useful' ends. On asking why that had happened, the director of the organization confessed that even though they had accurately identified the problem and the solution, they had not worked with the community itself to build and implement that solution. The community hadn't been part of coming up with the answer, even though they were the ones experiencing the problem. As the old African proverb says, 'If you want to go fast, go alone; but if you want to go far, go together.'"

"This is encouraging," Kim said. "But one of the reasons I don't think I'm naturally creative is that I usually find that others have already done what I want to do. That was one of the strongest critiques made by my college friends."

"This brings us to the third underlying skill for innovation," Roshan said, nodding. "The conventional notion is that innovation means coming up with something that hasn't been thought of or done yet. When it comes to social problems, however, most of our immediate ideas have likely been tried already—and failed. This is why those problems are still present. To come up with new solutions, we need to look at the problem itself differently. This is called **reframing the issue**.

"During a program I took at THNK, an executive school in Amsterdam that develops 'creative leaders,' my whole class gathered to help one member explore how he could attract more tourism (and thus, economic development) to his home country of Mauritius by looking at the problem in a different way. Eventually, we reframed the image of Mauritius from being a tiny and insignificant island chain in the Indian Ocean to being the largest 'ocean state' in the world. This required a radical change of perspective—or a *reframe*—of our conception of the country itself, because we were no longer looking at the islands (i.e., the land masses) but the entire ocean surrounding the few islands that make up Mauritius. In other words, Mauritius wasn't just the land; it was also the ocean. And that reframe—being the largest ocean state in the world—is something that a tourism department can work with!

"Reframing is thus about actively seeking out and challenging our default ways of thinking and our assumptions about how the world works, even if by doing so we risk looking foolish and ridiculous. When we're stuck on a problem, sometimes all we need is another perspective. This new perspective, or *frame*, can help us design a new solution."

"In fact," said Ilaina, picking up the baton as Punky dozed happily by her feet, "there is a history of changemakers consciously reframing problems to come up with elegant new solutions. Boyan Slat, a young Dutch innovator, recently built a company by reframing the answer to ocean pollution as not about how humans can clean up the ocean, but about how we can use ocean currents to let the ocean clean itself.

"When Gian and Sriram set out to help the slum-dwelling youth of Nairobi, they began where most well-intentioned people do: by asking how they can help give these youth a sustainable life. In that framing itself, note who is doing the giving and who is doing the receiving. This is a common mistake made by the novice changemaker. As they continued their *sensing*, they began to ask how they might give these youth the skills to earn money, which then leads to the inevitable idea that what young people in slums most need is vocational training to get jobs within the formal economy. During a feedback session when they pitched their idea, we asked them: 'this is what everyone does—how can you look at the problem differently? Instead of asking how you can help them, what happens if you ask, how can *they help you?*'

"It may have been easy to ignore that feedback. But for Gian and Sriram, it was finally the epiphany they sought. They changed, or reframed, their question to ask: 'how can we use the existing skills of youth in slums to help them earn money?' Like many of the best social change ideas, this flips the dynamic from seeing disadvantaged youth as victims of their circumstances to seeing them as active agents of their own progress. Gian and Sriram went back to the drawing board with this new question, which eventually led to the pioneering idea of running storytelling city tours of Nairobi led by street youth.

"When you change your frame of reference, you start asking different questions, and that gives you the path to finding different—and more creative—answers."

"Let's go even deeper with your question, Kim," suggested Roshan. "A common belief among those who study innovation is that there are very few truly new ideas out there. Nearly all creative ideas actually come from combining things from different arenas, in new ways. In other words, it's not about new ideas but new combinations. The ability to make new combinations, to connect the unconnected, is our fourth critical innovation skill, and it's often called **associating**.

"A classic example of associating comes from George de Mestral, a Swiss engineer who used to walk his dog in the Alps. On returning home from these walks, he frequently spent time pulling out burrs that clung to his dog's fur. He began to study the 'natural engineering' of these burrs and, after many years of trial and error, came up with something we now unthinkingly use every day—Velcro.

"The story of Velcro also points to a deeper insight. One of the most rarely used, and yet most available options to all of us, is to associate from nature. Through 4.6 billion years of evolution, nature is the ultimate problem-solver. So what, and how, can we learn from it, even if we're not an engineer like George de Mestral?"

Ilaina continued, "When starting Amani Institute, we learned about the field of biomimicry, which is about seeing how nature's designs can be applied to solving human problems. Besides Velcro, another example that you will enjoy, Kim, is a building complex in Harare designed by architect Mick Pearce. He used design methods inspired by indigenous Zimbabwean masonry and, most famously, the self-cooling mounds of African termites, which stay the same temperature inside no matter what the outside temperature is, even in the desert! The building has no conventional air-conditioning or heating, yet stays temperature-regulated year-round with dramatically less energy consumption.[34] Biomimicry has a rich set of such examples, but they are nearly exclusively in the domain of science and technology.

"In contrast, we realized that, in over a decade working in the social sector, we had never seen changemakers look to nature for insights on how to solve problems—not even those working in conservation. This is even more surprising when you consider that a major source of social problems is that our approach to human systems—like business, politics, and cities, to name just a few—seems so disconnected from how healthy ecosystems actually work. As we considered how to best train people in catalyzing social change, we were struck by how much value a greater engagement with nature might provide us."

"So how can those of us who aren't scientists learn from nature?" Farah asked.

Roshan responded, "We designed a course at Amani Institute called Bio-Empathy: Learning from Nature, specifically to help our students explore how they can tap into the wisdom

---

34   Jill Fehrenbacher, "Biomimetic Architecture: Green Building in Zimbabwe Modeled After Termite Mounds," *Inhabitat*, November 29, 2012, https://inhabit. com/building-modelled-on-termites-eastgate-centre-in-zimbabwe/.

of nature to unlock innovative approaches to social problems. We first encountered the word *bio-empathy* in Bob Johansen's book, *Leaders Make the Future*, where he describes it as a core competency of twenty-first-century leaders. But Johansen, like us, is standing on the shoulders of giants—from indigenous cultures throughout history through to Leonardo da Vinci, Antoni Gaudi, and the founder of the field of biomimicry, Janine Benyus.

"The course consists of two intertwined elements: The first is to learn from nature *as a mentor*, a guide or teacher, and to emulate how it goes about solving problems. The second element is to see nature *as a mirror*, reconnecting personally with nature to understand how it operates and using that connection as a source of inspiration to come up with new ideas. Both elements are intimately linked, and the course explores both simultaneously. Amani Fellows spend time reconnecting with nature through a number of immersive experiential activities, receive an introductory understanding of biomimicry theory, and then apply all they learn to addressing a local social problem."

By now, everyone was ready to move again. We packed away the picnic materials and stood up. Punky was already bounding away, ready to burn off energy after her nap. The rest of us descended the hill a lot slower. Kim, who was in the lead, suddenly turned around and asked, "What's the role of technology in all this? I'd previously thought innovation was all about making new inventions. In fact, my idea to tackle climate change involves home-brewing hydrogen to power houses."

"That's a common belief, perhaps driven by our pop culture's way of glamorizing Silicon Valley innovators," said Roshan. "But innovation is so much deeper than new technology, and this gets to our next skill, which we call **finding the flip**. I'd like to tell you a story.

"On April 3, 1973, standing on Sixth Avenue in New York City, an American engineer named Marty Cooper held a prototype mobile phone to his ear and placed the first cellular call in history. At the time, Marty led systems operations for Motorola's communications division. I was fortunate to interview Marty in 2010, a profound conversation I still revisit from time to time.

"'We changed the concept of the phone call,' Marty explained. 'Today, if you place a call and someone other than the intended recipient picks it up, you are surprised. Previously, that was the norm—because calls were made to places, not people. That was the fundamental problem with standard landline telephones.'

"Since I grew up in the era of the landline phone, this set off a lightbulb in my mind. Marty was right. When I was in high school, for example, and was calling a friend about homework, that ringing phone in my friend's home could have been picked up by my friend's mother, father, grandparent, or a sibling. Today, in the cell phone era, none but my friend would pick up the phone. And that's the primary reason why Marty's first cell phone call created a revolution in personal productivity that catalyzed enormous cultural change. The difference between calling a place and person was profound, as it turned out. 'Our phones trapped us at our desks,' Marty said. 'After 1973, we could be on the move rather than sitting around waiting for a call. As a result, productivity leaps. GDP skyrockets. Organizational and societal structures change forever.'

"Thus, one of the secrets to innovation is realizing what lies behind anything new. It's not about the technology itself—but rather what *shift in behavior* that technology makes possible. The bigger the shift, the bigger the impact. When you next come across a creative new idea or technology or organization, look for the insight behind the innovation to understand why it works. What is being flipped or shifted? For instance, Wikipedia's great insight was to see that all of us collectively know more about the world than any single group of encyclopedia editors—and we're willing to share our knowledge for free. Applying that insight essentially killed the former encyclopedia industry.

"Now let's extend that thinking to emerging technologies whose real societal impact is yet to be determined. What shifts do they make possible? Virtual reality holds the promise of radically improving empathy with those far away from us. With 3-D printing, we can imagine a world where every *thing* can be printed cheaply; how might that reduce poverty? If artificial intelligence can automate much administrative work, what possibilities does that hold for saving our time for more creative pursuits? And if driverless cars become common, or virtual working becomes the norm, the biggest shifts of those technologies may be less on car drivers and white-collar professionals, but rather on the very structure of modern cities, dramatically changing parking lots, gas stations, office rentals, luncheon restaurants, and so much more.

"Always look beyond the technology to the behavior it can shift. This is how you will understand how to create solutions that stick."

We had reached the bottom of the hill and were making our way slowly down the tree-lined path back to the park gates. There were more people now, and our pace slackened with the increased traffic.

"We have time for one final secret to innovation," said Ilaina. "We began by talking about how higher education only teaches students to critique, and not to build. This is unfortunate because building is not just about the action. As former Google engineer Tom Chi describes in his 2013 TED Talk, '**doing is the best form of thinking.**'

"When Gian and Sriram hit upon their idea for street-youth-led city tours, they were in a bar in Mathare slum with some of these youth. They decided to test out the idea immediately. They asked the youth to pretend they were foreign tourists and to play 'tour guide' through the streets of downtown Nairobi. 'We didn't go home and write a concept note and build a model,' Gian recalls. 'Just in ten minutes of walking with them, without wasting any time or money, we got so many insights that we built into the solution.'

"What Gian and Sriram were doing is called **prototyping**, a term from the field of product design that means to test your idea in the real world and get quick feedback to fine-tune the concept. What makes this hard to do—the reason Gian mentioned the temptation to build a model on paper first—is that first prototypes usually fail. But if you're going to be creative, you cannot be afraid of failure. Innovators need to adopt a mindset that views failure as feedback. From that perspective you realize that the faster you fail the better, because you have less to lose early on. The more time you spend trying to create the perfect product, the more you have at stake in case you do fail.

"There is an old saying that 'no business plan survives its first interaction with a customer.' When building Amani Institute, we developed prototypes that were highly successful as well as some that were total failures, like running an online course in 2012 without ensuring that we had consistent bandwidth speed. Both the failures and the successes taught us lessons we continue to apply when designing new programs, and none of those lessons could have been predicted beforehand. This principle can be extended to any number of fields. Just as you can't learn how to play tennis from reading a book on tennis and you can't become a writer without writing a lot, you cannot develop your innovation skills without trying to create."

A SKILL FOR EVERYONE

We had now reached the park gates and were standing outside, enjoying the last rays of Saturday sunshine before parting.

"This was such a fun way to spend a Saturday," said Farah. "One last question: are these innovation skills specifically for entrepreneurs like yourselves though?"

"Of course not," said Roshan. "These skills are absolutely applicable if you work in an organization, at any level. They can even be applied to the process of finding a new job or discovering what type of job you want."

"What do you mean?" asked Kim, intrigued by the thought.

"Well, *asking the right questions* and *living the problem* help you probe what issue or cause really matters to you and why, and *reframing* helps you see that problem in a unique way," Roshan explained. "Reframing can also show you how to see an already existing career opportunity quite differently than you've been seeing it so far. *Associating* helps you pitch how the skills and knowledge you gained from previous experiences can serve a prospective new employer, and perhaps you can show them how they can learn from nature too. They'd never forget that! *Finding the flip* can help you reevaluate organizations you want to join and examine if their work leads to the behavior changes in individuals and societies that inspire you. And above all, don't just sit there thinking about it; remember that *doing things*—trying, succeeding, failing—is the best way to learn and grow."

As Punky strained at her leash, despite everyone stooping to rub the dog's cheeks one last time, Ilaina summed up the day. "These behaviors and skills will make you a master problem-solver, a trait that every employer throughout your career will prize above anything else you bring to the table. Don't be that person who only points out problems without ways to fix them!"

ACTION AND REFLECTION

Act:

1. Pick a problem you are interested in helping to solve. Follow one or two of the steps outlined above to become an innovator. Bonus points for following them all!

2. Don't forget to prototype your solution!

Reflect:

1. Why is social innovation so important to building an impact-first career?

2. Would your best friend consider you to be more critique-oriented or more action-oriented?

3. What skills do you still need to increase your social innovation prowess?

6

WEAVING
A NETWORK OF
RELATIONSHIPS

We were coming out of a meeting one Monday morning when we received a message from Kim: "Red alert! I need your help. I'm attending a happy hour event about climate change on Wednesday evening, but I'm panicking. I know this is a great opportunity to make connections to find a job, but I have no idea what or how to do it. Can you help, please?"

As it turned out, we were planning to attend the same happy hour, so we agreed to help Kim navigate the evening. Farah was planning to attend too.

WHAT NETWORKING IS NOT

The event took place in an old manor house, with high ceilings and wooden floors, in the hipster part of town. Entering, we were immediately struck by a vibrant, almost festive atmosphere that contrasted sharply with our shy glances around the room. All four of us leaned toward introversion, so entering an event full of people was not in our comfort zone.

Roshan was the first to speak. "Just like for you, Kim, the word 'networking' raises many people's stress levels, because it often conjures up images of formal clothes and cocktail events like this one, awkwardly balancing a glass of wine on a plate of hors d'oeuvres with one hand"—Roshan pointed to a group of people doing just that—"while using the other to shake hands and hand out and receive business cards, all the while making stilted conversation with people who are trying to gauge whether or not you might be useful to them while not-so-furtively glancing around the room to see if the person they *really* want to speak to is free, so they can edge away from you toward that person. Sounds familiar?"

Kim and Farah nodded firmly. We exchanged a look of understanding.

"If this is what networking conjures up, you're not alone," Ilaina said. "As social enterprise leaders, we often have to attend such events. As introverts, we loathe them. After attending one such event in 2015, I texted Roshan to say I left early to go do *real work* and, only half-kidding, I asked him to please remind me never to attend another event like that again! In fact, when teaching about introversion and extroversion, we often tell our classes that we find it less nerve-wracking to give a speech in front of 1,000 people than to approach a group of three people we don't know at a conference happy hour!"

As someone stopped to say hello to Roshan, Ilaina took a sip of her wine and then leaned forward to emphasize her next point. "But this doesn't have to be what networking is about. For those who enjoy and shine in events like this, who find it natural to chit-chat with several different people about mundane things and yet come away with a key contact or resource, more power to them! However, the ability to 'work a room' doesn't necessarily make you a great networker. So, if you're more in our camp, rest easy. There are multiple other ways to become a great networker."

HOW TO NETWORK EFFECTIVELY

Kim finished off his salmon canapé and asked, "How do I effectively network then? Everyone keeps telling me it's going to be important for finding a job or building my own project."

Roshan returned to the conversation in time to hear Kim's question. "There are many guides for how to network effectively," he began. "A Google search will bring up hundreds of articles and several books and frameworks called networking canvases. These are all useful. However, what we'll share are some general principles and tips when it comes to building your global network."

Ilaina kicked off. "Networking is not about a cocktail event or happy hour, even though that's the first image that comes to many of our minds. It's about the painstaking effort to build relationships. And that doesn't mean amassing a gigantic list of connections, but curating a set of people who are invested in your growth and success, and vice versa. People often call it *network weaving*. And weaving isn't done in a rush; it takes time and careful effort. So rather than imagining the well-dressed happy hour with a hundred people, think about a casual coffee with one person, done a hundred times over several years.

Focus on coffees, not cocktails. "Every so often, you may do a fellowship program or pursue a graduate degree, where you get to know several dozen people very well because of the intimate nature of such programs. In these years, the size of your network will expand quickly. Otherwise, build your network slowly but meaningfully.

"The trick here is not the one-time coffee meeting; it's how the conversation you have leads to staying in touch, sharing ideas and information, and unlocking access to opportunities. It's about making introductions for each other, to other new people who may enrich that person's life. When you travel to where someone you don't know well lives, it's about making the time to invite them for a coffee or a meal even though you aren't close friends (yet). If they, too, want you in their network, they will accept your invitation. In other words, it's the intentional building of trusted relationships, one at a time, with people who want you to succeed because they know you, what you stand for, and what you're trying to achieve."

"This is so comforting to hear! In that case, can we just leave this happy hour and go grab a coffee?" said Farah, eyes twinkling.

"We could," said Roshan. "But let me ask what you think is so bad about being here. What's stopping you from talking with people?"

"For starters, I don't even know what to ask for," she replied.

"Let's talk about that," responded Roshan, to the sounds of clinking glasses and murmured conversations continuing in the background. "At its best, networking isn't about getting things from others. In fact, we believe the most powerful words in good networking are *How May I Help You?* Asking this question removes stress from the conversation; it takes the pressure off both of you. Most people are more comfortable doing a favor than asking for one, so lean into that. Help without thinking about a quid pro quo.

"When we were setting up Amani Institute in India, a family acquaintance reached out and mentioned how intrigued he was. He wanted to help. As he was a wealthy and well-connected leader with accomplishments in both business and social impact, I jumped at the chance to meet him. We met at his office and explored ways to work together. Then the man said what sounded like, 'Wiifm?'

"'Excuse me?' I replied, never having heard this expression before.

"'W.I.I.F.M.,' he repeated. 'What's in it for me?'

"I was taken aback. Perhaps the power disparity between us was less than I had imagined. I'd also never been asked this so bluntly as a pre-condition for help. I tried to politely disagree, saying that in my own experience, I benefited most when I did not think about WIIFM, but rather opened myself to *possibility*. Generosity usually pays back in the end. I left the meeting with a sour taste in my mouth. It was perhaps unsurprising that the man in question never actually helped Amani Institute in India, even though he easily could have.

"By contrast, I received a great lesson in networking when I met Britt Yamamoto, the founder of a family of social enterprises that focus on leadership development. During one of our early conversations, Britt rattled off a half-dozen ways he could help Amani Institute by making connections to potential donors and clients. Deeply grateful, and yet uncomfortable in the face of such generosity from someone I'd only recently met, I confessed that I wasn't sure what I could do in return to help him.

"Britt smiled gently and said, 'There doesn't have to be a quid pro quo. Perhaps you'll help me in the future, but there's nothing I want in return now.'

"Britt was essentially living out the credo: How May I Help You? Perhaps we should replace WIIFM with HMIHY—though I admit it has less of a ring to it—because this is what good networkers do. Ever since that conversation, Britt and I have built a strong friendship, and our organizations have collaborated many times, despite being as far apart as Seattle and Bangalore. HMIHY is how you build a web of goodwill, social capital, and trusted relationships—and Britt has these in spades. You might even call it good karma. And helping others not only feels good, it's also strategic because our careers are long, and we rarely know in advance what we need from our network or who will be the right person to help."

Farah was nodding along eagerly. "Let me try that!" she burst out, and disappeared into the crowd. Soon, the person who had wanted to leave the event was talking animatedly with a group of complete strangers. We watched her with a smile.

Then Kim broke in. "I still feel awkward when talking with someone new. I feel a need to pretend to be more interesting than I actually am. And I don't even know what help to offer them; I'm just starting my career."

Just then, Farah reappeared with a big grin. Despite our questioning, all she enigmatically said was "If it works out, I'll let you know."

Still curious about Farah's experience, Ilaina continued, "Kim just asked a question that takes us to the next principle. It's about **being yourself**, not pretending to be someone you aren't. When there's a power disparity between two people in a conversation, and you feel you're the one with less power, it's common to behave like someone you think your interlocutor would like, trying to seem smarter or more fun or well-connected. You do this because you fear the person might not like the real you. You fear rejection.

"However, many studies have demonstrated that authenticity is actually the key to meaningful relationships. In Brené Brown's famous TED Talk, she said that when people connect from a place of authenticity, they 'are willing to let go of who they think they should be in order to be who they are.'[35] How we show up in each interaction is very important, as it develops our reputation as dependable or well-connected or generous. Authenticity also positively impacts your well-being,[36] but that's a story for another day!"

"It sounds ideal, but not easier. I may be authentic and still have little to offer," objected Kim.

"Sometimes, it's as simple as speaking your truth and sharing your values," Ilaina replied. "As we discussed that day we met virtually, employers care a lot about who you are as a person. Your personal qualities play a major role in determining how well you do in your career. So even when you may not have technical skills to contribute, you can always utilize your soft skills while staying authentic to who you are."

Both Farah and Kim looked doubtful, so Ilaina continued, "There was a defining moment in my career when authenticity paid off big time. I had reached the final stage of a highly competitive selection process to represent Argentina at an international youth summit in Scotland. Along with my colleague, I'd traveled from my hometown in Cordoba to the capital, Buenos Aires, to present our ideas. After the pitches, there was

35 Brené Brown, "The Power of Vulnerability," filmed June 2010 in Houston. TEDxHouston video, 20:19, https://www.ted.com/talks/brene_brown_the_power_of_vulnerability/up-next.

36 Anna Sutton, "Living the Good Life: A Meta-Analysis of Authenticity, Well-Being and Engagement," *Personality and Individual Differences* 153, (January 15, 2020): 109645, https://doi.org/10.1016/j.paid.2019.109645.

a public vote to determine the winner. We were winning this vote until some people who hadn't been present for the pitches suddenly entered the room and voted for another candidate at the last minute. My blood started to boil from the unfairness. Outraged, I strode up to the organizer, a young woman whose name was Marina Mansilla. I don't get angry very often, but it's definitely better not to be near me when I do."

Roshan nodded vigorously at this. Ilaina punched him playfully on the shoulder and went on. "From a network-ing perspective, approaching someone when enraged is not recommended! However, I was very authentic, and Marina responded exceptionally authentically too. We had a great conversation, in which we resolved the situation. Since then, we've always supported each other at every step of our careers. In fact, Marina recruited me to Ashoka, which led to meeting Roshan and starting Amani Institute together. I know I can always count on her!

"Now, I'm not saying you should go around using anger to build your network"—Farah and Kim burst out laughing—"but that it pays off in the long-term to be honest about who you are and what you think. Being yourself takes way less effort than pretending to be someone else."

Kim looked amazed. "Networking is so much deeper than I imagined."

"And it's also more personal than I thought," added Farah. "However, even if I follow all these principles, my current network—basically my family and friends—can't help with my next career move since none of them have a clue about impact-first careers."

"You've touched on another core principle of good networking," Roshan said with a nod, "which is to actively build relationships with people on the periphery of your circles of contacts. Instead of 'best friends forever,' consider **best acquaintances forever.** We instinctively think of our 'network' as our family and friends, classmates, professional colleagues, and social and/or spiritual communities. While it's always valuable to invest in these relationships, it's also extremely important to reach out to those who may not be close to you at the moment. Herminia Ibarra, a management professor at London Business School, has written that your immediate network can also work *against* your professional growth because those people are invested in the 'current you' and may feel threatened by how the 'future you' may develop—possibly away from them.[37]

"If you're looking to make a significant career change—say, to switch from the private sector to the impact-first sector, as in your case, Farah, or become an entrepreneur, or take a job your family may not approve of, like you, Kim—your immediate circle of friends and family often holds you back. You need to find people who are further away from you presently, but closer to the new aspirations you hold.

---

37 Herminia Ibarra, *Working Identity: Unconventional Strategies for Reinventing Your Career* (Cambridge: Harvard Business School Press, 2004).

"It's what sociologist Mark Granovetter called 'the strength of weak ties.' Granovetter famously discovered that while most people indeed found new opportunities through personal contacts, those personal contacts were more likely to be distant acquaintances than close friends or family members.[38]

"So, as you consider those on the periphery of your social circles, you'd also benefit from doing a 'diversity audit' of your network. We live in an age where, on the one hand, diversity is increasingly a moral, strategic, and business imperative, and on the other hand, our social media and 'filter bubbles' push us toward ever-more homogeneous circles. But we gain so much from interacting with those who are different from us. Consider your professional networks: to what extent are the people in them from different age groups, nationalities, races, religions, political beliefs, socio-economic classes, and so on? How skilled are you at talking to people from very different backgrounds? Since important opportunities come from those with whom you have 'weak ties,' it's important to get to know those who don't look or think like you."

By now the happy hour was officially over. The music had stopped, and we realized we were the last people left in the old manor. Ilaina winked at Roshan. "This is the first time we're the last people to leave a happy hour!"

38　Mark S. Granovetter, "The Strength of Weak Ties," *American Journal of Sociology* 78, no. 6 (May 1973): 1360–1380, https://www.jstor.org/stable/2776392.

Laughing, we left the house and started walking down deserted streets illuminated by vintage lanterns that created the perfect aid to self-reflection. Add a little background jazz music and we'd be in a Woody Allen movie.

Like a falling glass that shatters the silence, Kim burst in with characteristic youthful energy. "I'm ready to become a networker! How do I start?"

That brought us out of our reverie. "Let's find somewhere still serving coffee," said Ilaina, "and we'll share some next steps."

HELPFUL NETWORKS YOU CAN CREATE YOURSELF

A couple of blocks later, we found an open café. When everyone had their hands around a warm mug, Roshan began to answer Kim's question. "Here are two types of networks you can actively create or join right away.

"First consider building your **Kitchen Cabinet**, a term that started with US President Andrew Jackson, who famously seemed to trust his informal network of advisors and friends more than his actual cabinet secretaries. Today, the expression means an informal group of people you can call upon for advice when needed. This 'cabinet' should be personalized and tailored to your needs. For example, you might think about who you would choose as your 'Minister of Career Advice,' or

'Minister of Love and Relationships,' or 'Minister of Personal Finance,' or 'Minister of Business Advice,' and so on.

"To begin creating your Kitchen Cabinet, reflect on what would be your most important 'cabinet positions' at the moment. Then, consider who you would assign to these positions.

"Here are five tips to keep in mind as you do so: First, they should be people you know well and can contact easily. Second, cabinet positions can be both temporary and permanent—some positions can change over time as your career or life progresses, while some will always remain the same. Third, some ministers can also provide general advice, as people whose opinion you trust broadly. Fourth, diversity is useful to get opinions from different perspectives. And finally, to take the pressure off, know that you don't have to bring them together in real life, and that these individuals don't have to know they are in your cabinet!

"Once you have the positions filled, here are five more tips for effectively managing this personal cabinet of ministers: First (and obviously), reach out to the relevant minister when you want to discuss an issue. Second, make sure you send a written thank you note after the meeting, and let them know what outcomes you've had based on their advice. Third, be in contact with each of them at least two to three times a year, keeping them informed about your life *even when you don't need their advice*. Most importantly, actively look for ways in which *you* can help them—it shouldn't be a one-way relationship (i.e., the HMIHY principle). Finally, don't pretend to be someone else; remember, these people care about *you* more than your job."

Kim nodded. "I already know who some of my ministers will be."

Ilaina continued, "Let's move to the second type of network. Making a career change, going against your family's wishes for a certain job, or taking the risk to start a new organization can be profoundly isolating, because sometimes our closest connections are the most resistant to our changing course. What helps immensely in these moments is to join a new *tribe* (in other words, your behavioral kin—people whose values or choices mirror your own) or **community of practice** (i.e., people doing the types of things you want to). Indeed, much research shows that if you want to create new habits, then joining a group that already practices those behaviors or life choices is highly effective because it gives you energy, makes you feel less of an outcast, and helps you follow in the footsteps of others who have already walked the path you're on.

"This is one reason why so many fellowships exist in the social entrepreneurship sector. Entrepreneurs find it remarkably morale-boosting to be around people who don't ask why they take such risks instead of settling for a stable job, who understand how their purpose is core to their identity, and who rejoice in seeing each other grow. And like social entrepreneurship fellowships, there are several other types of communities of practice that can help you along your way."

"Does the HMIHY principle also apply to your community of practice?" asked Farah.

"Absolutely! It's wise to contribute to your community of practice as much as you receive from it," Ilaina responded. "Aditi Agrawal, a young Indian changemaker, understands this instinctively. She was the first Amani Fellow from India. It takes strong courage and conviction for a twenty-one-year-old Indian woman to convince her family that she should travel to Africa for five months to do a fellowship program. After she graduated, Aditi returned to India to work in education. A few months later, Tito, an Amani Fellow from Kenya, shared a job posting with JUMP! Foundation. Aditi applied, and was soon moving to Thailand to work with JUMP! Foundation. When they later transferred her to Australia, she sought out members of the Amani community for advice on life in Australia.

"On other occasions, when she traveled to Spain and to China for work, she deliberately sought out Amani Fellows in those countries to make new friends and tap into their local knowledge. As Aditi says, 'Wherever I go, it's always on my agenda to find Amani people because it's the fastest path to meeting potential new friends.' That statement reveals how deeply she understands the value of investing in her community of practice. Her conversations with Jerry Zhu, an Amani Fellow she sought out in China, inspired her with the urgency she needed to start her current company, School of Future."

Farah interjected, "I read in the news how India and China have recently been confronting each other over territory, and that it's leading to negative impacts on trade and livelihoods. It's inspiring to have this example of how a young social entrepreneur from India was motivated by one from China!"

Ilaina beamed with pride. "That's the kind of outcome that makes us proud and grateful for what we do. But the story doesn't end there. As Aditi was starting her new organization, like any smart social entrepreneur, she tapped into her Amani Institute community of practice for support. Jessica Comin, a talented graphic designer from Brazil, responded to Aditi's request for design support and went on to develop School of Future's initial logo for free. Other Amani Fellows in India and elsewhere have introduced Aditi to potential partners, funders, and more.

"But this is no one-way street. Aditi has given back to the Amani community in countless ways. She has nominated several people to the program she completed, including her own sister-in-law! She has represented Amani Institute at public events and hosted marketing and outreach events in her hometown in New Delhi. And she has made useful introductions for several Amani Fellows with others in her networks. 'Within any network, there are people that *show up* and people that don't,' Aditi says. 'Those who show up both offer and get more help in the long run. I try to ask for help clearly and succinctly. And I try to give back as much as I can.' Aditi is a great example of someone actively using a global community of practice—in this case, the Amani Institute network—to deepen her impact around the world."

"You can apply the idea of a community of practice in other ways too," observed Roshan. "When I lived in Nairobi, I wanted to learn more about improv comedy because I believed it would improve my skills as a facilitator and trainer. But there were no easily accessible improv comedy groups in Nairobi at the time. I emailed several friends who might be interested in 'jamming' together and asked them to invite their friends in turn. Thus, a small group of people began meeting every other Friday night to practice improv comedy. Those evenings helped me build an enjoyable new skill, which has come in handy several times since then, even after I left Nairobi.

"Thanks to social media platforms, it's never been easier to bring together loosely connected people into a community of practice. And that's how one of my most valuable communities of practice got started. In January 2012, I saw a social media post about a new executive education school in the Netherlands that was recruiting its first class. At that point in time, Amani Institute was slowly taking shape as a concept—we hadn't yet developed our curriculum or program structure. Researching this new school, which was calling itself THNK: The Amsterdam School of Creative Leadership (now it's just THNK), it appeared to be well-funded and backed by impressive-sounding people. The participants who had already signed up looked intimidatingly accomplished.

"I threw in an application and was invited for an interview while I was on vacation. I left the interview impressed, knowing that if I was offered a place in the program, I would take it even though I'd have to use all my vacation time for the year to do it. Later that day, when telling my co-vacationer friend about the interview, he tried to discourage me from it. 'Why go through another program?' he said. 'You already have a Harvard degree and have learned so much at Ashoka. This may not add very much.'

"I replied that I wanted to do it for two reasons. Firstly, I'd be in the founding class of a well-funded program, which would immerse me in the journey that the first class at Amani Institute would go through. (Remember from our day in the park how valuable that is as an innovation tool.) And since we were starting Amani Institute with no funding or backing, I'd get a first-hand look at everything it takes to create and run a world-class program. The second reason was that nearly all of my network until then was in India and the United States. If I wanted Amani Institute to be truly global, this program would provide a new network with significant European composition.

"My friend shrugged. 'Seems like a waste of time to me. Ok, where are we going for dinner?'

"Despite my friend's skepticism, my hunch about THNK would be life-changing. The THNK program, and the incredible network it generated, was undoubtedly the biggest accelerating factor in Amani Institute's global growth. THNK's incredibly credentialed leaders helped us develop our curricula for multiple programs and shaped our thinking about the future of education, innovation, and technology. The wider THNK network contributed funding, opened the door to major funders and clients, hosted events, and became highly popular faculty members."

MEET A CHAMPION NETWORKER

"Wow!" Kim exclaimed. "I'll start looking for my community of practice as soon as I get home."

Shaking her head at Kim's indefatigable energy, Farah quipped "Well, I'll do so tomorrow morning after a good night's sleep."

Everyone laughed. "Speaking of sleep, let's get going," said Ilaina. "I'll share one final story as we walk to the bus stop."

We scraped back our chairs, cleaned up our table, and began walking toward the bus stop. Ilaina continued, "Our favorite example of global networking comes from Carrie Rich, the founder of The Global Good Fund. Prior to becoming a social entrepreneur, Carrie worked in a major healthcare corporation in the United States. She started as an intern, assigned the lowest-level jobs in the hospitals—pushing the snack cart, folding laundry, taking attendance, and so on.

"Carrie met the CEO of the company, Knox Singleton, while taking attendance in a meeting, and she wanted him to be her mentor. Still an intern, she persuaded the CEO's executive assistant to arrange a meeting to discuss how to live a life of purpose. As the meeting wound up, Carrie wanted to prolong the conversation because she knew her chances to talk to Knox again would be few and far between. She instinctively proposed that they write a book together about leadership in healthcare, in which she would interview him and all he had to do was talk from his many years of experience. Carrie and their co-author would record the conversations and do the writing. It was a classic example of HMIHY in action.

"Knox agreed and they began working together, having many conversations over several months. Carrie would never have gotten this much time with Knox otherwise. Through the book project, they built a strong mentoring relationship.

"But the story gets even better from here. For Carrie's twenty-sixth birthday, Knox challenged her to raise money for a cause she cared about: business for social good. Carrie sent an email to her entire network and raised several thousand dollars to develop impact-first leaders. Then Carrie was contacted by an anonymous donor who said he liked her idea and wanted to meet her. They met at a café in Washington, DC, where, to Carrie's utter shock, this man handed her a check for $1 million to be used to support high-potential young leaders committed to social good through business. Carrie returned to work, went to Knox's office, slammed the check on the table in front of him and said, 'Look what you did!' The health company CEO looked down at the check, then quietly reached for his own checkbook and wrote out a matching check for $1 million.

"With $2 million in seed funding, raised exclusively through creative networking, Carrie and Knox co-launched The Global Good Fund in 2013, which has gone on to help over two hundred entrepreneurs in forty countries create 2,800-plus permanent jobs in disadvantaged communities, raise over $100 million in capital, and positively impact nearly ten million lives.

"Carrie's network weaving doesn't end there. After being introduced to Roshan by a mutual friend, Carrie flew from Washington, DC to Nairobi to take an Amani course and understand
firsthand how we could work together. In Nairobi, the Amani
faculty member teaching the course Carrie attended just
happened to be one of the leaders of THNK. Carrie went on
to attend THNK and wrote her next book in partnership with
THNK's managing director. Meanwhile, she also became an
Amani faculty member and has significantly contributed to
Amani's community of practice by teaching fundraising to
dozens of Amani Fellows, hiring some of them, selecting others
into The Global Good Fund's network of social entrepreneurs,
and making The Global Good Fund a client of Amani Institute.

"Being a professional fundraiser, Carrie is far more comfortable at cocktail parties than we are. She even met her husband
that way! But the key to her success—and the myriad awards
she has won for her work—is the depth of relationships she
builds and the warmth with which she does so."

As Ilaina was finishing, the bus pulled up to the stop. We hugged
goodbye, and Kim and Farah waved through the window until
the bus pulled away into the night.

ACTION AND REFLECTION

Act:

1. Think of three to five people you'd like to bring into your network. Applying the principles of networking effectively, how would you go about doing so?

2. Create your Kitchen Cabinet.

3. Research and join one new community of practice.

Reflect

1. What will you do differently in the future when it comes to networking?

2. How might you increase your contribution to your current communities of practice?

7

OWNING
YOUR STORY

About a week after the networking evening, we received a text message from Farah: "I have good news to share! Are you free this weekend?" Roshan was playing in a cricket match that Saturday, and Ilaina was going along to watch. We invited Farah and Kim to watch as well. They were enthusiastic at the prospect, since neither had watched a cricket match before.

Roshan was already in his cricket uniform when Ilaina, Farah, and Kim arrived. The match wouldn't start for another hour, so Roshan suggested climbing the bleachers where there was a nice view of the whole ground. As we sat down, some of the other players began arriving and warming up. Curious to hear Farah's news, Roshan called out that he would join them later. Farah could barely contain herself anymore. "Do you remember when I went to talk with people at the happy hour after our conversation around leading with HMIHY? In one group, the conversation turned to how difficult it is for NGOs to find high quality yet affordable designers. One person mentioned that he urgently needs someone to design the fundraising campaign for a program that works with at-risk children. With your advice ringing in my ears, I volunteered to help with the design. Last week, I spent every spare minute on the project. The director liked my work so much that he then introduced me to five peers in other organizations in case any of them also needs support. One of them has asked for a meeting in her office next week—they are apparently hiring a full-time designer! I'm so excited because it could be my first big break to move toward an impact-first career."

"Congratulations!" everyone cried out simultaneously.

In the field, the distinctive sound of a cricket bat hitting a ball carried over to us as players started to practice fielding drills. Then Farah frowned. "But I'm nervous. I struggle when I think about how to introduce myself and how I might fit into their organization. It's a unique opportunity and I don't want to screw it up. Can you help?"

CAREER NARRATIVES AND STORYTELLING

Kim spoke up. "I've heard that storytelling is a good tool to connect with others. But I'm not sure what storytelling means in this context."

"That's some good associating, Kim!" said Roshan with a wink and a smile. "Career narratives—and personal brands— thrive through storytelling. A personal narrative can be far more effective in helping you connect to potential employers, employees, collaborators, or other members of your network, than the traditional analytical communication we're used to. A good story creates an emotional connection between you and your audience, allowing them to remember it, identify with it, and share it with others.

"As I mentioned when we met online, I studied under Dr. Marshall Ganz in the early days of Barack Obama's unlikely run for president in 2008. Ganz had developed a technique, based on over thirty years of working in community organizing across the United States, for telling stories that move people to take action. Ganz applied this technique in the Obama campaign with a transformative effect. He's since been credited as the mastermind behind the campaign strategy that led to the record voter turnout that elected America's first black president. So, if you've heard of the value of storytelling as a professional skill any time in the last decade or so, then chances are the trail leads back to Marshall Ganz. His propagation of the tool, through his students' subsequent work (ours included), has spawned an industry of books, TED Talks, consulting firms, and professional story coaches."

"What's the fuss about?" Kim asked. "Why is storytelling so effective?"

"Human beings interpret the world in two ways: through analysis and through narrative," Roshan continued. "As Ganz teaches, analysis uses critical reasoning and data to teach us how to act or what to do about something; by contrast, narrative uses story and emotion to teach us how we *feel* about things, which in turn tells us *why we act.*[39] Unfortunately, we've been educated to rely on analysis to persuade others, despite mounting evidence that people are more effectively moved by stories. In the last decade, several other thinkers have confirmed Ganz's insights and extended the research on storytelling into fields like neuroscience, behavioral economics, healthcare, and so on.[40]

"When it comes to getting people to act, the most brilliant piece of analytical reasoning is no match for a well-told story. Take, for instance, Jacqueline Novogratz, who founded Acumen, one of the world's leading impact investing firms. To demonstrate the interconnectedness of humanity in today's globalized world (and thus our obligation to help others less fortunate), she could present a data-rich economic analysis about international trade and the flows of goods and services.

"Nobody would remember a word of it.

"Instead, in her book *The Blue Sweater,* she tells the story of how a sweater that pictured zebras grazing in front of Mount

---

39 Marshall Ganz, "Public Narrative, Collective Action, and Power," in *Accountability Through Public Opinion: From Inertia to Public Action,* eds. Sina Odugbemi and Taeku Lee (Washington, DC: The World Bank, 2011), 273–289.

40 See the works of Daniel Pink and Paul Zak.

Kilimanjaro was her most beloved piece of clothing throughout middle school. After a classmate made fun of Novogratz
for wearing the now-ill-fitting sweater during high school, she
donated it to charity. Ten years later, Novogratz was working
in Rwanda when she saw a young boy wearing the exact same
sweater. She ran over to him and looked at the sweater's tag.
Sure enough, her name was there, in faded black ink.

"This story makes the same point about the interconnectedness of humanity in the modern economy as a presentation on
trade flows would, but in a much more memorable way. Like
Novogratz's name in faded black ink on the sweater's tag, the
story leaves an indelible image in our minds. We won't forget
it in a hurry."

"That is a good story indeed," said Farah. "The designer in me
can already see how to create an effective campaign around it.
But how do I apply this to my own career?"

Ilaina took up the baton. "To position yourself for an effective
career in changemaking, we believe that applying storytelling
skills to how you communicate can give you a major boost. For
instance, let's say you just graduated from an undergraduate or
graduate program, like Kim, and you want to align your degree,
internships, extra-curriculars, and work experiences to pitch
yourself as a great new employee. Or let's say you're making a
significant career shift from one industry or sector to another,
like Farah, and you wish to reinterpret your professional track
record to help you flow into your desired future career. Or
perhaps you want to quit a stable job to start your own new

organization. In all these cases, a well-told story about your career so far makes it easier for others to accept and support your choices, by helping them make sense of what may look like quixotic decisions in the light of where you want to go now. A good narrative also helps potential employers, partners, and coworkers get to know you better. Finally, and even perhaps most importantly, your career narrative can explain your choices to *yourself* as much as to others, and give you a firm understanding of why you're changing direction."

"Can you share an example of that?" asked Kim.

Roshan glanced down at the field to gauge how much time he had before he was needed by his team. He then said, "Actually, one of our colleagues, Arjun Sashidhar, demonstrates how a career narrative helps explain your choices to yourself and your family and extended network, with an example from his own career prior to joining the Amani Institute team. At that time, Arjun was contemplating quitting his job as an instructional designer and moving back to a people-facing role in training and development. A defining moment came while helping another colleague resolve a career dilemma. Wait, let me read you the email he shared with us recently."

Roshan fished out his phone and began scrolling through. "Ah, here it is. Arjun wrote: 'I created online courses for corporate training, as an instructional designer. I loved my organization and had great teammates and mentors. My projects earned the company good revenue and clients were happy with my work. However, I found more fulfillment when making certain contributions that were outside the scope of my official responsibilities. My project manager would seek my help in resolving team conflicts. The HR department would turn to me for ideas on team building and employee engagement. I mentored and helped new team members find their footing. Over time, this made me wonder where I was creating my biggest impact. One day, a new team member who was having a hard time settling into her role reached out for help. At the end of our conversation, she said, "Arjun, you should be a motivational speaker, life coach, or facilitator. More than all the technical writing you do, it's who you are that's making a difference to people!" Thus, in helping her find a solution to her problem, I found a solution to mine. This insight cleared the path for my journey to Amani Institute.'"

Roshan put away his phone and began to do some stretches to warm up. Ilaina smiled at that, and continued. "Arjun's story is a classic career-change narrative. While he wasn't explicitly seeking an impact-first job—as you heard, he wanted to switch from online instructional design to coaching and facilitation— the skills he'd developed over the years were just as valuable in Amani Institute's social change work as another type of job. Not dissimilar to Farah and graphic design. Now Arjun gets to apply his passion for coaching and facilitation to train future generations of social change leaders. And his narrative helps both himself and those around him understand how he got there."

"That's such an inspiring example for me," said Farah excitedly. "In Arjun's story, I see elements of my own gradual realization that I could be doing more meaningful work with my design skills. When I was doing the project for the NGO, I physically felt more engaged, more *alive*, than I do in my office."

Ilaina nodded. "Absolutely! A good career narrative helps you see your career in a different light, which gives you a consistent way to speak confidently about your skills and interests."

THE BASIC PRINCIPLES OF ALL STORYTELLING

"I understand the *why*," said Farah. "But *how* do I prepare a career change story for my interview?"

Ilaina winked. "Well, by now you know that of course we've got some guidelines for you! As we mentioned, there are loads of books, TED Talks, and courses out there to help you master storytelling. To get you started though, here are some essential storytelling principles, which can serve as a foundation beneath any written or oral communication, be it your LinkedIn profile, a job interview, or your eventual TED Talk (yes, we're ambitious for you!). Call it Storytelling 101.

"To begin, it's vital to **make it personal, showing why you are doing it**. One of the most common questions we get as adults is 'What do you do?' An even better question, to ask yourself or someone else, is *why* do you do what you do? This leads to fascinating conversations and insights. As Simon Sinek famously argued in his viral TEDx Talk, 'People don't

buy what you do, they buy why you do it.'[41] Many people hesitate to talk about themselves or their motivations, but without
that information, nobody will 'buy' you because they don't
understand you very well. And when people don't understand you, they make up a story about you anyway. It's how the
human mind works. So why not proactively give them the story
they need to understand you? You've got to put yourself into
your story.

"That said, don't make things up. Authenticity matters—as
we discussed with regard to networking. Your story should be
true. Humans generally have good bullshit detectors, so if you
come across as inauthentic, it will significantly hurt your credibility."

A warmed-up Roshan plopped back down. "Next up is **the
story structure**. Despite its current vogue, storytelling is as
old as humankind. We're all steeped in it: our religious tradi-
tions, sporting events, family histories, literature and cinema,
music, politics, and so on, all revolve around stories. Think of
any classic story you know, and you'll see a common three-
part structure to all of them." He held up three fingers and
began to count down. "All stories consist of, first, a character
or set of characters (known as the protagonist), who must,
second, solve a problem (called the story's plot) wherein they
face a challenge and make a choice about how to deal with
that challenge. Third, they experience an outcome (the moral

---

41 Simon Sinek, "How Great Leaders Inspire Action," filmed September 2009 in
Puget Sound, TEDxPuget Sound video, 18:02, https://www.ted.com/talks/simon_
sinek_how_great_leaders_inspire_action?language=en.

of the story), which gives us, the audience, an emotional payoff and teaches a useful lesson. If you ensure your stories follow this three-part structure, your audience will be happy because humans are conditioned to process the world this way."

Ilaina held up a hand. "But don't get overly caught up in the structure either. The expression **'show, don't tell'** is our third principle of storytelling. Like all art, storytelling works best when you conjure up a scene or an image in your audience's mind and then let them interpret that scene. Sticking too close to the structure can push us to connect the dots for the audience. But you should resist that urge. Instead, provide details that appeal to the senses: what the weather was like when your story happened, what people were wearing, what they looked like, and what they could see, smell, and hear. This will help paint a picture in the audience's mind and make them more likely to go where the storyteller wants them to.

"*Believing* and *feeling* the story at a personal level is critical because ultimately we act based on our emotions, which in turn are driven by our values. We rarely act based on intellectual reasoning. For effective storytelling, you must **connect with what the audience believes about itself**, or show them why they should care. Nothing moves us to act more than when we feel threatened, inspired, compassionate, or empowered—emotions that are at the heart of taking action. This is the hardest part of storytelling, where you help the audience understand what's in it for them when it comes to helping or following you.

"Any other principles?" Ilaina finished, looking at Roshan.

"One more," he said, twirling a cricket ball in his hands as a thinking aid, tossing it from palm to palm, absent-mindedly playing catch with himself. "You're much more likely to get a favorable outcome when you **make it easy for your audience to say yes** to you. The key to getting that yes is to ask the audience to do something specific. There's a huge difference between a generic request to 'support Syrian refugees' or 'share my CV with people' versus a highly specific 'go to ABC website right now and make a donation to their refugee camps in Jordan' or 'please share my CV with your friend at X organization because they have an opening that fits me.' The second examples give the audience a clear idea of how to act; the first ones don't."

DEVELOP YOUR CAREER NARRATIVE

As Farah and Kim nodded, Roshan continued. "In fact, opportunities to effectively use stories abound—they aren't just for giving a speech or hosting a dinner. You can effectively deploy them in just a minute or two, to start off a staff meeting, break the ice at a networking coffee, discuss an issue with a colleague, or connect to a community you want to help."

"Got it," said Farah. "And let me see if I can put this together for my upcoming interview. I'm guessing that regardless of what media of storytelling I'm engaging in, a compelling career narrative must first explain why I am reinventing myself and my career. Second, it should explain who I want to become or

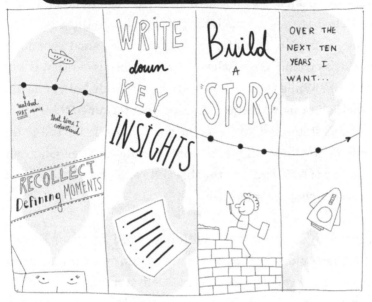

what impact I want to create. Lastly, it should share ideas about opportunities that will help achieve our collective vision."

"Very good!" Ilaina exclaimed, as Roshan exchanged a fist bump with Farah. "Now that you know what to include, you can build a story using these four simple steps. Step one is to recollect some life events or defining moments that made you reconsider what type of career you'd really like to have. Revisit your signs of awakening, as we discussed when you attended our class on aligning who you are with what you do. Step two involves writing down the primary insights you gained from these moments that point the way toward your ideal career.

"Step three is to build a story about how these insights helped you move from a low point to a breakthrough. Remember that we all love stories in which the protagonist (in this case, you!) comes through to win after a struggle. For instance, remember our Swiss friend, Gian, whose story we discussed that day in the park? While their initial research had only led to conventional solutions, when he and his partner reframed their initial problem statement to focus on what youth from the slums could do for them, they had a breakthrough. When Gian tells the story of Nai Nami, it's that breakthrough insight that tends to stick in people's minds.

"Finally, in step four, close with how you'd like your story to end. This could be at the end of your career, over the next five or ten years, or even just what you'd like to accomplish in the next year. The time span of your story can vary depending on circumstances, but it should leave the audience with a clear view of the promised land, which is the impact or moral of the story."

HOW TO SHARE YOUR CAREER NARRATIVE

Roshan got up to join his teammates as the game was going to begin soon. Just then, Kim spoke up. "I'm really happy for you, Farah, that you got this interview. But can I get some tips too? If I don't have a specific event, like an interview, to prepare for, how could I be more proactive in getting my story out there? Is there a way to use my story to bring people to me, as opposed to only sharing it when I meet them?"

Ilaina placed a hand on his arm in understanding. "It's smart to be proactive about sharing your story, as it can act like a magnet, making it easy for those who want to find you. Let's move beyond direct sharing, such as when you are speaking, and focus more on indirect storytelling. Or, in other words, to influence what people find about you online. Just as good investors know how to make money even when they're on vacation, good storytellers leverage online media to share their career stories widely."

Roshan had picked up his cricket kit and started to walk down the concrete steps of the bleachers but paused and turned around. "And this is not just a nice-to-have! It's wise to craft your online career narrative because of one simple fact: you *will* be Googled. By prospective employers or employees, clients and partners, people you're about to meet for coffee or who you just met at a conference, and so on. We all live in the open now. As blogger Chris Betcher writes, 'In the future, your "digital footprint" will carry far more weight than anything you might include in a resume or CV.'"[42]

"I don't mean to keep you from your game," said Kim.

Ilaina laughed. "Don't worry, he feels really strongly about this. Go on," she encouraged Roshan to continue.

Roshan looked over his shoulder to his teammates and gestured

---

42 Chris Betcher, "Footsteps," *ChrisBetcher.com* (blog), May 14, 2009, http://chris-betcher.com/2009/05/footsteps/.

that he would be joining shortly. Still standing, he began. "There are three primary media through which you can tell your career story. I share them in order of strategic importance.

"Always begin with **your LinkedIn profile**. This is the *only* career narrative platform that's absolutely essential these days. You must have a well-crafted LinkedIn page, if only because it's a little suspicious when you *don't* have one. This is the go-to place for everyone who wants to learn more about you professionally, or introduce you to someone else (it's so much easier than asking for your CV), or stay informed about your latest endeavors. Therefore, your LinkedIn profile needs to be an active record about who you are as a professional."

"What's the best way to use my LinkedIn profile to share my career narrative?" asked Kim.

Roshan continued, "Here are three basic but necessary things to do. First, include a header that makes people curious about your professional identity and what you're looking for in the future. Second, add a summary that backs up the header with a story about your journey, your choices, the impact you've made, and what you can bring to your future role. This can be just two to three sentences—it shouldn't be several paragraphs long. For example, my summary is something like this: 'Right after finishing college, I turned down a traditional job to work in social impact. Ten years later, I co-founded Amani Institute to help others do the same all over the world—build lives and careers where they don't have to choose between making a living and making a difference.' As you can see, the narrative describes the arc of my career story and my long-term professional passion, rather than listing my work experiences and educational background. Your summary should catch people's attention and make those with similar values eager to connect with you. If you have a personal mission statement, this is the place to include it. And the last step is to request testimonials from peers, colleagues, and mentors who can endorse your story.

"The second medium is to develop an **online portfolio**, a personal website that tells your story in ways that a LinkedIn page and certainly a CV or a resume cannot. Your CV focuses on basic facts like where you studied, where you worked, and your key accomplishments in quantifiable terms. By contrast, your portfolio is a valuable complement to your CV, as it helps people understand *who* you are and the *value* of your accomplishments in visually pleasing ways.

"While an online portfolio is useful for everyone, it is especially critical for freelancers and consultants to have one. It provides examples of the impact you've had in a much better way than a traditional CV ever can. It's also particularly valuable for those who do multiple things at any one time—for example, you may be a graphic designer *and* a facilitator *and* a public health expert, and you may want to be open to short-term opportunities in all three domains. Nothing helps you showcase this better than an online portfolio.

"Today, there are several platforms, both free and paid, that make it very easy to build a personal portfolio or website, even if you have no coding skills. This field is also rapidly evolving and there are more sophisticated platforms emerging constantly.

"And remember to apply storytelling principles to make your online portfolio stand out!" Everyone smiled at Roshan's conviction, even when he clearly needed to go.

"I'll take it from here," Ilaina said, shooing him away. "Good luck in the game!" The others echoed her good wishes, and Roshan ran down the stairs to join his team.

"There's one more set of options to proactively share your story," Ilaina continued, leaning back against the bleachers, turning to face Kim. "Besides LinkedIn, other **social media and publishing platforms** heavily in use today include Facebook, Instagram, YouTube, Medium, and TikTok. And, as with portfolio building, there are new platforms emerging constantly. We understand that not everybody needs (or likes) to use their personal social media accounts for professional purposes. However, if your network on any of these platforms is valuable for your professional goals, or if you want to position yourself as a thought-leader or expert by sharing your knowledge with the world, then these platforms are valuable because you don't have to go through the trouble (and the rejections) of pitching ideas to editors and other gatekeepers. If you choose to share professional content on them, don't forget to use our storytelling principles while crafting your posts to make them memorable and compelling, leading to action."

EXPECT THE UNEXPECTED

"I feel more prepared now, even though *I* don't have an interview to show off my fancy design skills," said Kim with a cheeky grin.

Farah ruffled his hair and put on a faux-maternal tone. "Your time will come, little one. Don't you worry!"

Ilaina added, "And once you begin sharing your story, you'll be surprised at how many opportunities seem to suddenly appear—often, things you couldn't have predicted in advance. Take a wide-angle view on what emerges and follow any trails that appeal to you. In addition to job opportunities, you may also make new friends or learn about interesting education programs. I even know people who met their future spouses this way! One day you'll look back and see how the dots connect, how your story was emerging all along, and how you just had to keep the narrative going to get to the ending."

"And that's the moral of *this* story, isn't it?" Farah remarked. "That we should own and define our career narratives so that others can easily understand how best to help us or work with us."

And with that, they all turned to face the field as the game got underway.

ACTION AND REFLECTION

Act:

1. Using the four-step process outlined in the Develop Your Career Narrative section, connect the dots of your professional history into a narrative about your impact so far and future aspirations.

2. Identify which platform you want to share your career narrative on and make a first attempt there. Bonus points for trying a different platform than the one you typically use. For example, if you have a robust LinkedIn profile, then consider creating an online portfolio.

Reflect:

1. Reviewing your career narrative, what new insights have you gained about your story?

2. What new opportunities or signs of awakening might those insights be pointing toward?

8

REALIZING IT'S
A MARATHON

The following Saturday, we were due to attend a prestigious awards ceremony for the "Social Entrepreneur of the Year." We had two extra tickets and invited Kim and Farah to join us. On Saturday evening, we entered the building, which had decorated the walls with posters of various social entrepreneurs' work around the world. Light jazz wafted around the attendees sipping coffee or soft drinks while waiting for the auditorium doors to open.

Waiting in line for our drinks, Farah turned to us. "In your work with all these leaders around the world, have you seen any trends or patterns in their lives? If Kim and I successfully build impact-first careers, what can we expect to experience along the way?"

TRAVELING THE INNER JOURNEY
OF THE CHANGEMAKER

"Indeed, changemaker journeys can often follow a similar pattern," Roshan remarked. "We've seen this repeatedly, not just in the lives of great global leaders like Nelson Mandela, but also in leaders working tirelessly at the community level, whose names you'll never know. We have seen it in our own lives as changemakers. And you can see this path reflected not just in modern leadership literature,[43] but also in ancient paradigms like 'The Hero's Journey'[44] and even in the lives of spiritual leaders like Jesus, Mohammed, and the Buddha. Putting all these inputs together, we mapped five phases of the inner journey. Each phase asks different questions that help us navigate our journeys at our own pace. This is one of the centerpieces of the 'Inner Journey of the Changemaker' course, the one you both attended at Amani Institute.

"First, as we discussed in class, is **"Awakening,"** which asks *why do I want to create change?* Understanding your initial awakening and desire to contribute toward a larger purpose both anchors you and drives you forward, helping you stay true and focused during your life as a changemaker.

"Then comes **"Exploration,"** which asks *what are my options?* Once you know the source of your motivation, you begin a phase of learning, of sensing what the world needs and how

---

43   See the work of Otto Scharmer and Peter Senge, to name just two.

44   "Hero's Journey," Wikimedia Foundation, last modified June 8, 2021, 15:32, https://en.wikipedia.org/wiki/Hero%27s_journey.

that intersects with your own interests. It's important to listen to your inner voice as you examine the needs of your community and the world. Your strengths, weaknesses, and core skills all come into play as you seek remunerative work that contributes to the change you want to see in the world. Gradually you come to know what you must do."

We reached the bar and picked up our drinks. "That's the stage Farah and I are in now, correct?" Kim said, leading us to a quiet corner where we could talk.

"Yes," Roshan confirmed. "Our conversations to-date have been to help you explore your options to build an impact-first career. However, since we complete several cycles of the inner journey, there might well be several phases of exploration throughout your career."

Ilaina took over. "The next three phases come after you've gotten a good sense of your options. The third phase is "**Decision**," which asks *am I ready to jump?* People who've dedicated their lives to changemaking often have a story about the actual moment they decided to take a leap of faith and start walking their talk. Regardless of whether you're born with privilege, the temptation to choose the safe option is a legitimate barrier. Starting a dialogue with yourself and those you love takes courage and commitment. The "Decision Phase" can mean switching careers immediately or honing a craft and gathering new experiences for a while before making the leap.

"The fourth phase is "**Action**," which asks *how do I make my vision come alive?* Tackling complex problems requires persistence and patience. Impact-first work often brings more setbacks than victories. The slow pace of genuine change requires caring for yourself and monitoring your energy to avoid exhaustion or cynicism. Practices of renewal such as sport, art, travel, and spirituality help immensely here. The point is to build the resilience and stamina to 'stay in shape' while doing the work."

"But how do we do that?" Farah asked. "What builds this resilience or helps us stay in shape, as you put it? It sounds easier said than done."

"We'll get into that too," replied Roshan. "To round off the journey, the last step is "**Transformation**," which asks *who have I become now, and what's next?* You see, as we try to change the world, the world changes us in return. Sometimes we change so much that we realize we must move on to a new project or career, which then constitutes a sign of Awakening, and the cycle begins anew. But this time you carry with you all the experience and tools from previous cycles of the inner journey. The "Transformation Phase" also helps us reap the harvest of our work, in the form of lessons and insights to share with others."

Just then, a loud gong clanged and the lights in the hallway dimmed. The event was about to start. As everyone lined up to enter the auditorium, Roshan quickly added, "It's especially important to note that this is not a linear cycle, one step at a time. There may be moments when you must go back before moving forward. The time to pass through one phase can vary widely from person to person, from a matter of hours to several years. Creating change is a continuous journey of discovery, which is part of what makes it both powerful and enjoyable."

We found our seats and made ourselves comfortable. The stage was abuzz with activity; light and sound technicians were doing their final checks. Then they all cleared the stage and the auditorium darkened, only the stage still lit. The master of ceremonies, or MC, came on and welcomed us. He screened a series of short videos that presented the work of the ten finalists for Social Entrepreneur of the Year. In each video, the social entrepreneur narrated their origin story, connection with the cause, impact their organization had achieved so far, and how they had gone about their work. After these videos and some speeches, the MC announced a thirty-minute interval before they revealed the winner.

As the lights came back on, Kim remarked, "It's incredible and inspiring to learn about all these people who've been working on the same social problem for two or three decades."

"Absolutely," agreed Farah. "I can't imagine how they have sustained themselves for so long! As I asked outside, how is it possible to ensure we stay resilient and motivated over time?"

THRIVERS AND SURVIVORS ON THE CHANGEMAKING MARATHON

"Let's get into that now," said Roshan. "One of the most over-looked aspects of impact-first work is that it's like a marathon, not a sprint. No social problem will be 'solved' in a couple of years or with a quick fix. You must prepare for the long run. The "Action Phase" of the inner journey is the trickiest of the five phases. So many talented and committed people abandon the race because they aren't properly prepared for it; others keep running but stop enjoying it, just thinking about the finish line. And yet there are others who seem to be able to run one marathon after another."

Ilaina now leaned forward. "When we consulted with global experts while building the Amani Institute curriculum, many confessed that their organizations had become a burden, diminishing both their happiness and their impact. Many got divorced because of their work; others no longer believed the world could become a better place. These stories got me wondering why some changemakers feel exhausted and always on the verge of physical and mental exhaustion, while others seem hopeful and happy with their lives. A few years ago, I pursued a master's in Applied Positive Psychology at the University of Pennsylvania to try and understand this. Based on my research, we designed a dashboard to help people navigate the twists and turns of this marathon journey of changemaking, survive the bumps in the road, and enjoy the beautiful vistas they will pass along the way. In other words, to sustain themselves and their impact across decades. We need thriving changemakers over the long haul, not social impact martyrs.

"The dashboard has eight variables that spread across a continuum. Depending on your response (a definite yes or a definite no) to the question each variable poses, you might find yourself closer to the extreme right—*thriver*—or closer to the extreme left—*survivor*."

"What do you mean by thrivers or survivors?" asked Farah.

"Thrivers believe their work is worth pursuing because they are making a difference in people's lives. We've already discussed how people who work from a sense of purpose, as thrivers do, tend to be more productive, committed, motivated, and efficient, have more positive relationships, and above all, are

SURVIVOR Vs THRIVER

MOVE The SLIDER to WHERE you CURRENTLY ARE.

No — Are you intrinsically motivated? — YES

No — Do you have enough positive relationships in your life? — YES

No — Are you explicitly choosing the life you lead? — YES

No — Are you living an integrated life? — YES

No — Are you aware of what you can and cannot change? — YES

No — Are you celebrating enough? — YES

No — Can you retain but not become overwhelmed by your empathy? — YES

No — Are you taking care of yourself as much as you take care of others? — YES happier. On the other hand, survivors may be deeply committed to their cause (or not), but can't seem to find happiness. They enter a vicious cycle where they experience negative job satisfaction and performance and see declines even in their overall life satisfaction, but still don't quit their jobs. Survivors experience more negative than positive outcomes from their social impact work."

"Gosh, well, I really want to know how to thrive!" exclaimed Kim. "Do I need to start thinking about that already or only after many years working toward social impact?"

"Prevention being better than the cure, it's wise to consider this issue from the beginning and not when you're burning out," said Roshan.

A DASHBOARD FOR YOUR INNER JOURNEY

"Let's start right away! What's the first variable on the dashboard?" asked an animated Farah.

"The first question to answer is: **are you intrinsically motivated**?" began Ilaina. "This is about the source of your motivation. In general, changemakers act because they feel a deep connection with humanity and/or the planet and want to do something to improve the status quo. They recognize that their motivation isn't primarily linked to money or status, but to living out their calling. Impact-first professionals are *internally* driven, which is called intrinsic motivation. When someone is intrinsically motivated, they come closer to reaching their potential and being happy with their work and their lives."

"It's like trying to quit smoking or exercise more," added Roshan. "You're much more likely to succeed if you are intrinsically motivated and not driven by an external incentive. Any external incentive—say you're exercising because you want to look good for beach season—can work for a while, but once summer is over, you regress to your old self."

"I get that," said Farah, and Kim nodded as well.

"However," continued Ilaina, "sometimes we *think* we're acting from intrinsic motivation but are either not identifying our motivation accurately or masking our true motivations. The most common ways this happens in impact-first work are the motivations to avoid guilt, feed our ego through external recognition, and heal our own wounds. This is a trap you should avoid."

Kim and Farah reflected on this. Then Farah remarked, "I can relate to that. I feel very privileged for all the opportunities I've had and at the same time slightly guilty because other women don't have them."

Nodding in understanding, Ilaina continued. "Feelings of guilt due to our privilege is something we've heard repeatedly over the years. Privilege isn't just about economic status but also comes from educational backgrounds, skin color, gender, the loving family we had, or even unfavorable life events or circumstances that allowed us to learn and grow rather than falling apart. We're born with some of these privileges, and you cannot escape a privilege once you have it. No matter how much someone tries to deny their past, or donate their inherited wealth, the privilege remains. What you *can* decide is how to relate to your privilege."

"How might we do that?" asked Farah, intrigued.

"Some people protect their privilege for generations," Ilaina went on. "This isn't the case with changemakers, many of whom are driven by their privilege to want to change the world. However, once we recognize our privilege, there are different ways of relating to it. Some changemakers feel guilty, even ashamed that they 'have so much,' and often this drives their motivation to act. While that motivation may be well-intentioned, acting from guilt can have negative consequences down the road. For instance, the changemaker unintentionally begins to behave in a paternalistic way, since he or she is also working to relieve their own feelings of guilt and shame. They start to imagine they are acting *for* or acting *on behalf of* instead of the more effective acting *with*. As a famous quote sometimes attributed to Lilla Watson goes, 'If you have come to help me, you are wasting your time. But if you have come because your liberation is bound up with mine, then let us work together.'"

"I know what you mean," said Kim, looking a bit rueful. "I once volunteered at a slum and found myself pitying the people living there, like I needed to save them from that situation. Now I understand I was putting myself above them. I must confess it felt good at the time. And yet, even then, I knew I was doing it more for me than for them." He covered his eyes with his hands in shame.

"Don't be ashamed, Kim. On the contrary, being able to identify what you thought and felt is a rare skill," said Roshan.

"What about external recognition?" asked Farah, sweeping her hand to indicate the plush auditorium. "Events like this for example. In my current company, our motivation is supposed to come from the goals we set for ourselves, but meeting those goals doesn't bring me lasting satisfaction. In fact, it leads to a rollercoaster of emotions driven by the numbers."

"This also happens in the impact-first world," Roshan noted. "It's very common for people to drift from their intrinsic motives and start being driven by salary increases, climbing the title hierarchy, appearances in the press, summing up the funds they have raised, awards they have won, their likes and followers on social media, and even tracking obsessively the number of people they've impacted. Those types of numbers may be good indicators or goals, but they shouldn't be the real drivers of our actions—the reason we wake up every morning to work—or it will start to feel stale after a while."

"And what about unfavorable or painful life events, as you alluded to earlier?" Kim reminded us.

"Yes, a traumatic event or psychological 'wound' can also confuse our intrinsic motivation," Ilaina acknowledged. "One of our colleagues, Geraldine Hepp, a founding staff member of Amani Institute, describes what's called the 'wound-gift concept,' in which someone decides to work on a social problem because they have suffered themselves from that problem; sometimes, perhaps without noticing, what they're really trying to do is to heal themselves. Most social entrepreneurs have a personal story linked to the challenge they are facing. This is not wrong; it's often very helpful to be personally affected by your cause. For instance, remember Jerry White, who taught us about aligning who we are with what we do? He transformed a life-threatening wound into a gift for the world: instead of submitting to the trauma of stepping on a landmine and losing a leg at the age of twenty, he joined his personal struggle with the International Campaign to Ban Landmines, which eventually won the Nobel Peace Prize in 1997. However, when we act *from* the wound itself, then emotions like sadness, anger, and hate will drive our actions. By contrast, through his own 'work' in overcoming the trauma, Jerry created a framework that helps victims of any tragedy move from seeing themselves as a victim to a survivor to eventually a leader.[45] That's what

---

45 Jerry White, *Getting Up When Life Knocks You Down: Five Steps to Overcoming a Life Crisis* (New York City: St. Martin's Press, 2009).

we mean by the wound-gift concept, which has been with us throughout history. You can trace it from Dante's *Inferno* to modern TV shows.[46] In other words, you don't need to step on a literal landmine; there are plenty of metaphorical land-mines in our lives. How to create a gift for others from your own personal 'landmine' may sound like alchemy, but by going through the process of healing, you develop the inner strength and insight through which you can support others and inno-vate new solutions grounded in experience."

"Putting all this together, acting from intrinsic motivation seems similar to having a clear purpose," reflected Kim.

"It's more about asking why it's *your* purpose, why you of all people have that purpose," clarified Ilaina. "Understanding our intrinsic motivation means asking specific, not generic, ques-tions. A generic question would be: why do you wish to work in education or to prevent malaria? A generic answer—'because malaria is bad' or 'children should be in school'—obscures a proper understanding of your convictions. What truly moti-vates *you* to prevent climate change, Kim? You need to dig deeply for clarity of purpose."

---

46 An example comes from the TV show *The West Wing*, written by Aaron Sorkin. It goes something like this: a man's walking down the street when he falls in a hole. The walls are so steep he can't get out. A doctor passes by and the guy shouts up, "Hey doctor, can you help?" The doctor writes a prescription, throws it into the hole and moves on. Then a priest comes along and the guy shouts, "Father, can you help me out?" The priest writes out a prayer, throws it into the hole and moves on. Then a friend walks by. "Hey Joe, it's me, can you help me out?" And the friend jumps into the hole. The guy says, "Are you stupid? Now we're both down here." The friend says, "Yeah, but I've been down here before and I know the way out."

The lights turned off again, and the winner of the Social Entrepreneur of the Year award was announced. She had built an organization to empower local efforts for climate change mitigation in many cities. She stepped up on stage surrounded by her family and her team. We all stood to give them an ovation.

"Let's hope she's driven by intrinsic motivation," whispered Kim. "I'd hate to see her burn out before she has the impact we need her to have!"

As everyone sat down, Roshan commented, "By seeing all those people with the winner, you just witnessed the second principle for thriving. Thriving changemakers acknowledge that an important source of motivation, inspiration, and resilience are the people in our lives, who provide moral, in-kind, and even sometimes financial support. Therefore, ask yourself: *do you have enough positive relationships in your life?* These relationships happen at several levels: family, friends, support networks, and teammates. These supporters are not necessarily related to our work themselves but nevertheless become great supporters and admirers of the mission. As we discussed at the networking event, it's also extremely valuable to have a support network from the changemaker community, so you can share the peculiarities of the journey with others in similar situations.

"Finally, if you can't connect with the people around you, it doesn't matter how much impact you strive for. It's critical to connect authentically with others, even if only for a few seconds. Jane Dutton of the University of Michigan calls these 'high-quality connections,' daily interactions that may seem small and insignificant, but are marked by mindfulness, positive mutual consideration, trust, and active participation on both sides.[47] In a high-quality connection, people are more open to learning and have better cognitive functioning, creativity, commitment, and, above all, health and happiness. It's easy to focus on the desired impact and forget that much of the motivation we need comes from making high-quality connections on a daily basis."

As Roshan finished, the MC was handing the microphone to the winner. She began her speech by thanking everyone who had supported her thus far, confirming what Roshan had just said. She then added that she was ready to walk each step of her journey all over again if needed, despite the sacrifices she made along the way.

Upon hearing this, Ilaina leaned across to Farah and Kim and whispered, "Most leading changemakers accept that they will sacrifice time with their families and financial rewards to realize their impact. This brings us to the third variable: *are you explicitly choosing the life you lead?* Sacrifice is neither bad nor good. The important thing is whether the sacrifice is consciously or resentfully made. Common phrases such as, 'I have to work this weekend because there is a deadline on Monday,' or, 'I can't take a vacation when

---

47   Jane E. Dutton, *Energize Your Workplace: How to Create and Sustain High-Quality Connections at Work*, (Hoboken, NJ: Jossey-Bass, 2003).

there are people who need my support,' or, 'I must go to this meeting even though I'm sick because it's a unique opportunity,' demonstrate an admirable sense of duty. However, it would be very different to say, 'I *choose* to work this weekend because the deadline is Monday,' '*I don't want to* go on vacation when there are people who need my support,' or '*I want to* go to this meeting no matter how sick I am, because it is a unique opportunity.'

"The difference between the two types of statements reflects one's level of autonomy. Autonomy is a major driver of life satisfaction. When you *have* to do something, it's often because you think something is expected of you—and you lose autonomy. When you *want* to do something, you get to own your decision. When we speak of 'wanting to' instead of 'having to,' our sense of autonomy is restored. And there's always the possibility to choose our path, even in the worst circumstances. As Viktor Frankl, a psychiatrist, philosopher, and writer, describes in his famous book *Man's Search for Meaning,* 'everything can be taken from a man but one thing: the last of the human freedoms—to choose one's attitude in any given set of circumstances, to choose one's own way.'[48] When you consciously choose to sacrifice your weekend, you start enjoying the process itself. 'Working on a weekend' thus becomes a 'day without distractions.'

"But note that we are neither advocating for nor against working over the weekend. We just want you to consciously choose

---

48   Viktor E. Frankl, *Man's Search for Meaning,* (Boston: Beacon Press, 2006).

your life's path and accept the consequences. Sounds like our winner really understood this principle," finished Ilaina, still whispering.

The speeches were over; we could talk normally again. Farah asked, "Are you talking about work-life balance?"

"It's more about asking, *are you living an integrated life?*" answered Roshan. "When you decide to build a career around a social cause, an interesting thing happens: the mind-space you give this cause grows so much that it's almost the only subject you can talk about anymore. If you've ever gone out with friends and couldn't help but talk about your amazing job, it's clear that work is starting to play a central role in your life. This is known as the 'centrality of work,' or the importance someone attributes to work in terms of their life as a whole.[49] Accepting that work is central to their lives can be liberating, as changemakers often feel judged by other people for the time they dedicate to their jobs and, by implication, the time they fail to dedicate to other aspects of their life.

"To be clear, work centrality is not a problem in itself. Once again, it's a choice. However, there is a difference between centrality and exclusivity. Exclusivity is an addiction to work that leads to negative results, such as worse job performance,

---

49   Irina M. Paullay, George M. Alliger, and Eugene F. Stone-Romero, "Construct Validation of Two Instruments Designed to Measure Job Involvement and Work Centrality," *Journal of Applied Psychology* 79, no. 2 (1994): 224–228, https://doi.org/10.1037/0021-9010.79.2.224.

lower life satisfaction, decreased mental and physical health, and toxic personal relationships. For many 'survivors,' it can be difficult to understand who they are outside of work.

"In less extreme cases, we come across the concept of work-life balance. But this is a trap. Talking of a 'balance' between work and life implies a trade-off or a zero-sum game, as if life does not include work. Many changemakers feel a need to choose between 'my family versus my mission' or 'a meaningful job versus financial well-being.' When you fall into this kind of binary thinking, life gets more stressful. You begin to feel guilty, that what you do is never enough, that you're always missing out on important events. You feel off-balance. On the other hand, if you reframe it as work-life *integration,* then there's no false dichotomy, since your work and personal life are complementary, not competing, priorities.

"Indeed, Stewart Friedman, professor at the University of Pennsylvania, has found that successful people integrate the different spheres of their life: self, home, work, and community.[50] In other words, your work is part of your life and thus must be integrated, not separated. It also means that if all you do is work, without looking at other spheres of life, things go awry. For instance, if you neglect your health because you're too busy at work, the resulting negative health outcomes will reduce your productivity. Once you understand that it's both

---

50   Stewart D. Friedman, "What Successful Work and Life Integration Looks Like," *Harvard Business Review,* October 7, 2014, https://hbr.org/2014/10/what-success-ful-work-and-life-integration-looks-like.

possible and necessary to integrate different spheres of your life, then you see how things like spending time with your family or practicing your hobbies ultimately also enriches your social impact."

At this point, the president of the organization managing the award ceremony came onstage to congratulate all the nominees. He used hard data to show the impact achieved by the ten finalists: "Collectively, they have lifted more than a million people out of poverty, given education to three hundred thousand children, planted one million trees..." and so on.

As he spoke, Farah asked, "These numbers are incredible—so many lives changed forever. And yet, I can't help thinking, is it enough? Given how much is still left to be done in all of the finalists' fields of work, can they legitimately feel proud of those numbers?"

"People working for impact are professionals, but not heroes," Ilaina began. "I met an education entrepreneur who confessed he used to send emails at 4:00 a.m. and expected his staff to reply by 6:00 a.m. because 'we have to help the suffering children.' If his team didn't respond right away, he felt disappointed. Today, after working for twenty years at this pace, he believes that this behavior positions him as a hero who gives everything for his work, which can be very harmful because he cannot educate every child with his organization's limited resources. In reality, an army of people across all sectors of society is needed to solve each social problem. If poverty does end, it will be because of the work of multiple organizations and sectors. Conversely, if poverty remains with us, it's also not the fault of any one individual or organization.

"To help our students understand this, we teach an adapted version of the model created by Stephen Covey, best known for his book *The 7 Habits of Highly Effective People*. In this three-circle model, the inner circle shows what you can change in the world, or your area of control. The second circle shows what you can influence but not control. And the third circle shows what you can neither influence nor control."

"It's like the famous Serenity Prayer," said Kim, and he quoted Reinhold Niebuhr's famous line, 'God, grant me the serenity to accept the things I cannot change, courage to change the things I can, and wisdom to know the difference.'"

"Exactly!" said Ilaina. "It's important to ask, **are you aware of what you can and cannot change**? Thriving changemakers are clear where the limits are of what they are trying to achieve, and where they can be most effective and impactful. They know where their circles of control and circles of influence start and end. They understand that theirs is a part of the contribution of a larger group of people, all striving for the same goal in different ways. When you take on unlimited responsibility, like 'fighting poverty,' you're up against a seemingly immovable system. Your motivation decreases and your frustration increases. Your resources to change the world are limited, and therefore, it's wise to establish goals that are challenging but doable. Don't try to do it all!"

"And this leads to the next question on the dashboard, **are you celebrating enough**?" added Roshan. "Changing the world is a never-ending marathon. Except in rare situations like eradicating a disease, there is no finish line where we declare total victory. We need to celebrate every kilometer of the marathon, else we'd never have the energy to keep going. Celebrations generate positive emotions like joy, awe, and gratitude, which all lead to better work, physical and mental health, social relationships, happiness, and even income. Celebrate when you achieve what's within your sphere of control, even if things aren't going well outside your sphere of control. And don't skimp on celebrations—this isn't the place to save money! In fact, events like this award ceremony are a celebration for all of us, not just the winners," said Roshan, noting a celebratory vibe growing in the auditorium that was evident to all of us.

Up on stage, an emotional video was screened, in which the beneficiaries of the finalists' work gave testimonials about the impact they'd had. Huge smiles and not a few tears abounded both in the video and throughout the auditorium.

As soon as the video ended, Ilaina turned to Farah and Kim. "Did you know that empathy is almost an inherent attribute of changemakers? However, you need to manage it carefully, which is the next variable in the dashboard: **can you retain but not become overwhelmed by your empathy**? According to Paul Bloom, professor of psychology and cognitive science at Yale University, there are many definitions of empathy, so he distinguishes between two main terms: sympathy and compassion.[51] He defines sympathy as 'the ability to put yourself in the other's shoes and feel what you think they are feeling'; whereas compassion is the 'ability to care about others' well-being, but without necessarily feeling their pain.' It's very common for changemakers to be moved by the context that surrounds them, which usually means the presence of people in distress. Those who feel the pain of others for a long time may come to suffer from *empathy fatigue*, a gradual decrease in compassion over time, which makes them lose hope and motivation with regard to the cause they've been fighting for.

"Furthermore, an excess of sympathy can lead to decision-making guided only by strong emotions and not rationality, even decisions that may be morally wrong. By setting limits on our empathy, we are better able to critically analyze situations and solve problems more efficiently."

"I've always wondered whether empathy is a blessing or a curse! Now I understand it can be both; we need to learn how to manage it," said Farah.

The event ended and the celebratory cocktail hour began. Kim and Farah approached the winner to ask her perspective on thriving versus surviving, and how to avoid burnout. When they returned, they said she had responded with just a question: **"Are you taking care of yourself as much as you take care of others?"**

---

51 Paul Bloom, "Empathy and Its Discontents," *Trends in Cognitive Sciences* 21, no. 1 (January 1, 2017): 24–31, https://doi.org/10.1016/j.tics.2016.11.004.

"What do you think she meant?" asked Farah.

"Just go into any bookstore," responded Ilaina, "and you'll find entire shelves on the importance of self-care: sleeping well, eating well, exercising, etc. However, although most change-makers recognize the risk of burnout, they aren't always great at taking care of themselves. 'I'll sleep more next month,' or 'I'll exercise more next year,' is a common refrain. This para-dox—of changemakers not taking care of themselves despite knowing its importance—can be understood when you rank their priorities. For many changemakers, their main priority is the *other*; their own needs come second.

"By contrast, thriving changemakers prioritize both themselves *and* the other. They understand there's an interdependent rela-tionship between themselves and others, so the best thing they can do for their long-term impact is to preserve themselves."

Roshan continued. "Changemakers also often de-prioritize themselves financially. Many take huge financial risks that eventually force them to 'drop out' of the marathon because they can no longer sustain their family. It's vital to make an income that allows for a decent life. Otherwise, you'll always worry about money, taking your focus away from the impact.

"Beyond finances, prioritizing both yourself and the other also means taking breaks for rest, setting limits on your availabil-ity, and spending time with loved ones without feeling guilty. Changemakers need to understand the close relationship of self-care with social impact."

The cocktail hour was now in full swing, a live jazz band getting everyone's feet tapping as they tucked into scrumptious hors d'oeuvres. The joy and sense of possibility filling everyone was tangible in the air. "Imagine if we could have these award ceremonies not just for social entrepreneurs but for changemakers working in government, businesses, educational institutions, and every community," Ilaina speculated dreamily.

Roshan nodded. "The world would be a better place, and we'd feel much more fulfilled in our careers."

ACTION AND REFLECTION

Act:

1. Identify which stage of the Inner Journey of the Changemaker you're currently in, and why?

2. Consider the eight questions on your marathon dashboard. Identify in which ones you're naturally a thriver and naturally a survivor.

Reflect:

1. Now that you know an impact-first career is akin to a marathon, what concerns you about your "fitness" for such a career?

2. How can you improve your ability to sustain an impact-first career over the long haul, knowing there'll be a deep fulfillment from the impact you create?

9

CONCLUSION
Walking Our Talk

Dear reader,

In the first version we wrote of this concluding chapter, we continued the conversation with Farah and Kim, but one year later. We described how Farah got promoted to lead an entire country office of the organization she was interviewing with in Chapter 6, and how Kim discovered a passion for using sports to promote social impact, a field much different than climate change. But then we decided it was time to say goodbye (and good luck!) to Kim and Farah, and turn instead to you—for you are the star of the story to come, once you put this book down.

But first, here's an update on the two of us. We're writing and publishing this book in the year after we stepped down as leaders of Amani Institute and transitioned the organization to a new leadership team. At this point, neither of us knows what our next challenge will be. We are in the Transformation Phase of the Inner Journey of the Changemaker, closing one major cycle of our lives and preparing to enter the Awakening and Exploration stages in the near future.

This means that we'll get to follow our own advice on how to build an impact-first career. Although we don't know how it will play out, and so much may yet change along the way, here are some examples of how we'll be walking our talk, following the six keys:

Let's start with the first key: *designing your own education.* How do we plan to keep improving our skills, following the six principles of holistic, experiential, challenge-based, contextual, engagement-based, and reflective learning?

Ilaina, for example, is currently coaching people in impact-first careers. This allows her to keep mastering her leadership and communication skills. To enhance this work, she is reading more and taking short courses. She's also part of several advisory councils and boards, to keep learning alongside impact practitioners. Regarding technical skills, she's learning French because new languages open up whole new worlds. And she's also engaged in reflective learning through her first Vipassana Retreat, ten days of silent meditation to connect deeply with herself. She clearly believes in the value of life-long learning!

Looking at the second key: *aligning who you are and what you do*, are we looking for new signs of awakening? Reframing our purpose? In short, what's our new alignment?

Roshan sees his career to-date in distinct phases. Over the first decade, he worked to support some of the best social entrepreneurs around the world. For the next decade, he brought those insights into career development, helping future leaders build impact-first careers that can change the world. For him, alignment in the next phase involves taking insights from both social entrepreneurship and leadership development to address a specific cause he cares about, though he's not yet sure which cause that is—perhaps it's around sustainability or the future of democracy. As he "awakens" to his new calling in another field, he knows his purpose may also shift slightly.

Moving to the third key: *becoming a social innovator,* how will we keep mastering the skill of social innovation?

We're fortunate; we know *how* to come up with new ideas. For instance, within sustainability, Roshan is increasingly passionate about sustainable travel. Travel is his favorite hobby, even on par with cricket! One reason he believes travel is so important is a quote from Mark Twain: "Travel is fatal to prejudice, bigotry, and narrow-mindedness." Throughout Roshan's life, he's seen firsthand the truth of that line. And in a world where prejudice and bigotry seem to be rising, travel could be a critical tool to combat them. But travel also has a bad reputation these days, with people worried about the industry's carbon emissions. While travel still only accounts for a small fraction of atmospheric carbon, it's also one of the few sources of carbon emissions that ordinary citizens can control; hence, many advocate for reducing air travel. And yet the very people eco-conscious enough not to travel are those more likely to choose eco-friendly destinations when they do. Without their travel dollars, there's simply no hope for eco-tourism, little chance to save gorillas, and orangutans, and elephants, and jaguars. Thus, sustainable travel seems to be ripe for innovation. For now, Roshan is trying to "ask more questions" and "live the problem." For him, that Mark Twain quote points to a connection between travel and the future of democracy. Perhaps there's a "reframe" somewhere there that will help "find the flip" on this issue. It's also worth noting this doesn't mean he must start a new organization—he can take these insights into a range of other organizations.

As for the fourth key: *weaving a network of relationships*, how will we network or join new communities of practice?

For Ilaina, the skills of social innovation and networking intersect. To deepen her innovation skills, she wants to interact with people outside of her echo chamber. After working with social innovators for many years, she wonders if she's lost sight of how the majority of people think and what they really want. She wishes to better understand other communities, like those disenchanted with the current political or economic system, those who don't believe in universal human rights, or those that simply don't want an impact-first job. She will begin by reconnecting with people in her own network she hasn't spoken with in many years simply because they followed different life paths.

Coming to the fifth key: *owning your story*, how are we going to tell our stories moving forward?

You've already read Roshan's reframed career narrative—how each decade of his career was building toward the next. And while this story may evolve as he comes to see the last two decades through different lenses, that career narrative is already on his LinkedIn profile. Furthermore, in a networking "coffee conversation" recently, someone in his Kitchen Cabinet suggested that he publish a few blog posts on sustainable travel or the future of democracy so prospective employers or collaborators can learn about him and reach out with ideas for "how he may help them."

We're sure you now see how the different principles within the different keys intertwine with each other. Once you're clear on your alignment, it's easy to own your story and network with the people who can help you pursue your desired impact-first career.

Finally, the sixth key: *realizing it's a marathon*, what will we do differently for the next phase of our marathons?

From the marathon dashboard, Ilaina really wants to focus on the first two variables to ensure she is thriving. First, she wants to be more conscious about acting from intrinsic motivation. When you're in the spotlight of leading an organization for a decade or more, it is not unusual to yearn for drivers of extrinsic motivation. Ilaina will spend time detoxing from being in the spotlight before she takes on a leadership position again. That's one of the reasons for her meditation retreat—she wants to learn how to reconnect to her intrinsic motivation faster whenever she gets distracted. Second, she wants to prioritize important relationships by spending more time with old friends. While she's dedicated a lot of time to her family and to those friends linked to Amani Institute, she's not spent as much time as she would like with friends in other circles. She wants to invest in those (and new) friendships too.

A SEVENTH KEY:
SAY 'YES' WHEN CHANCE COMES KNOCKING

We will harness the six keys while moving into the next phase of our careers because we know it's possible to intentionally build an impact-first career, to plan each step to get where you want to. Yet, we've often seen that *unplanned* things can take us in completely different directions.

For instance, when Roshan launched a peacebuilding program at Ashoka, he never imagined it would lead to him leaving to start a new organization. Similarly, if Ilaina hadn't accepted an opportunity to help Ashoka in Argentina on top of her other responsibilities at the time, she wouldn't have started working there eventually. And of course, when the two of us first met in Roshan's office at Ashoka, that summer day in August 2010, we didn't dream of creating a new organization together, let alone in Kenya, nor expanding it to three continents. In fact, unlike Ilaina, Roshan had no meaningful background in the field of education prior to Amani Institute. And yet he's now often invited to give talks about the future of education! All this happened only because we embraced unexpected opportunities, and it completely changed the direction of our lives. In fact, Celia Cruz, our Brazilian leader from Chapter 2, stressed that the most important part of building her impact-first career was seeing opportunities others hadn't.

To see such an opportunity, you need to be present in the moment, not distracted by all the other things you need to do. That's the first step to stepping on a better pathway. However, just seeing an opportunity isn't enough. It's easy to pre-judge an opportunity as something we aren't looking for, or we might be too scared to take it on because of all the changes it may imply in our life. We need both curiosity and courage to accept an unexpected opportunity without knowing exactly where it will take us.

Over the years, many people have remarked how "lucky" we were to find each other. Having the ideal co-founder is a rare thing indeed. However, while we're grateful to the universe for putting us in each other's paths, we believe that, as others have noted, luck is when preparation meets opportunity. By designing our own educations, being conscious of our alignment, mastering our innovation skills, networking authentically, sharing our stories (with each other first), and girding for our impact-first career marathons, we were in fact preparing to *get lucky*, as it enabled us to both see and unlock an opportunity we'd never dreamed existed.

Therefore, our seventh key involves being open to the possibility that things might happen differently than we imagined or planned. It's realizing that if we're clear about the purpose of our work, we can be open to that purpose taking on different forms—in our case, quitting our jobs to move to Kenya to start a social business! You might think of purpose as a source of intrinsic motivation that pushes us to act in alignment with who we are, but in ways that keep changing across the duration of our career.

TEN YEARS LATER:
THE NEW REASON TO WORK

These six—or rather, seven—keys will help you build your dream impact-first career. But remember, as we discussed in Chapter 1, the larger context is that all work is becoming impact-first, and all careers are becoming impact-first careers.

We envision that, in the future, when you apply for a job after university, your prospective employer won't ask for your grades as much as what impact you've already had in the world. We believe that all companies, no matter how big or small, will have to be able to explain how they are making the world a better place. We've noted the rise of social innovation departments in corporations, universities, and large NGOs in recent years; we see this trend continuing, eventually becoming as central to our education systems as literacy and mathematics. And we'll know that things have changed when parents bring up their children to aspire to impact-first careers over Ivy League universities or blue-chip companies, or rather, that prestigious universities and companies will be those that are explicitly trying to make a positive impact in the world.

Finally, to acknowledge the historic time in which this book was written, we believe that the COVID-19 pandemic will accelerate some of these shifts. Despite all the suffering, the pandemic has highlighted what we've achieved as a civilization, as well as indicated how much progress we still need to make on issues like inequality and climate change. And yet it's also reminded us that we are all connected and must solve our problems together. We predict that, in the next ten years, humanity will have changed how we perceive ourselves (more altruistic than egoistic) and realize the best way to solve problems (collectively rather than individually). This, in turn, will make all work impact-first.

AN INVITATION

We'll close by wishing you an impact-first career. We cannot promise you an easy journey. As Gandalf warns us in *The Lord of the Rings*: "It's a dangerous business, going out your door. You step onto the road, and if you don't keep your feet, there's no knowing where you might be swept off to." No less evocatively, when Nelson Mandela died, marketing guru Seth Godin wrote that Mandela's lesson was, "If you don't wish the journey to be easy or safe or comfortable, then you can change the world."[52]

But if you do step onto the road of an impact-first career, one that can change the world, if you join the uncountable millions of us crafting this new reason to work, then we can certainly

---

52 Seth Godin, "A Legacy of Mandela," *Seth's Blog* (blog), December 5, 2013, https://seths.blog/2013/12/a-legacy-of-mandela/.

promise you a transformative journey: for yourselves, the organizations you work for, and the world we live in. The most fulfilling way to discover the extent of your potential is through making the world a better place.

We'll be cheering you every step of the way. In addition, we're also here to support you, or help you brainstorm. Don't hesitate to reach out when you need to—nothing makes us happier than seeing people follow their impact-first passions.

Bon voyage!

—Ilaina and Roshan

ACKNOWLEDGMENTS

Our gratitude transcends this book since a nonfiction book is, in reality, the fruits of a life lived and things done. So, we first thank our parents—Mary Braganza and Alberto Rabbat, Lily and Mathew Paul—who showed us how to see the world with our own eyes and march to the beat of our own drums. Likewise, we thank our sisters—Celeste Rabbat and Nidhi Howell—and extended families for encouraging us to do this work. To the family we chose ourselves, deepest thanks to our life-partners, Ivan and Meeghan, for always supporting us and motivating us to walk our talk.

Having spent two decades each in the impact-first sector, there are innumerable changemakers we consider role models, friends, and mentors. Several are featured in this book, and there are so many more around the world from whom we've learned much of what we've written here.

It takes a special mission to bring an Indian and an Argentine together to start an organization in East Africa. From the beginning, we sensed how beautiful and impactful Amani Institute could be. We're grateful beyond words to the entire community of staff (past and present), Amani Fellows, other program alumni, faculty, partners, donors, and advisors who make it the very special world-within-a-world that it is. This book truly would not exist without you all.

Several people read early drafts and provided generous feedback to improve the final product. Heartfelt thanks to Aditi Agrawal, Teresa Chahine, Gaurav Dewani, Zaakir Essa, Francesca Folda, Caroline Gertsch, Stephanie Haase, Geraldine Hepp, Shehzia Lilani, Raiana Lira, Andrew McBride, Julia Melo, Anne Miltenburg, Pauline Ndonga, Arjun Sashidhar, Jerry Sellanga, Shriya Sethi, Rodolphe Strauss, Sumanth Suri, and Robert Wolfe.

Special thanks to Lucila Sarquis who poured dedication and passion into designing the lovely illustrations throughout the book.

Thanks also to Dr. Mary Gentile at the University of Virginia, one of the first people to believe in this book's potential and advise us in important ways. Other important advice came from Christian Busch, Julia Dhar, Ben Keene, and Anam Zakaria—thanks for sharing your wisdom before we even got started.

At Scribe Media, we'd like to thank Neddie Ann Underwood, and the rest of the wonderful team of designers, editors, and more, for keeping us on track and shepherding our labor of love into the light of day.

Finally, thank *you*, dear reader, for pursuing an impact-first life. This book would not exist without you.

ABOUT THE AUTHORS

AMANI INSTITUTE

Roshan Paul and Ilaina Rabbat are co-founders of Amani Institute, an award-winning global social enterprise which has, to date, helped nearly ten thousand people from over sixty-five countries accelerate their careers in social impact. Under their leadership, it has also supported more than 250 organizations around the world, from large global UN departments to small local businesses, and everything in between, to increase staff capacity, motivation, and impact. They stepped down as executive leaders of the organization in 2021 but remain active board members. In 2019, they were both named to the DO School's Top 25 Influential Leaders in Purposeful Organizations.

ROSHAN PAUL

Prior to Amani Institute, Roshan worked with Ashoka for a decade, where he designed and launched programs that supported over five hundred social entrepreneurs (Ashoka Fellows) around the world. Raised in Bangalore, India, Roshan has a master's in Public Policy from the Harvard Kennedy School and a bachelor's in International Political Economy from Davidson College. He has guest-lectured or spoken at conferences at over fifty universities and other institutions around the world, including Harvard, Dartmouth, Georgetown, and the World Bank. He has also conducted dozens of workshops at leading organizations from Vodafone to Oxfam, and Deloitte to UNICEF.

Roshan currently serves on the Board or Advisory Council of several innovative educational organizations in the USA, Netherlands, and India. He served a term on the World Economic Forum (WEF) Global Future Council on Behavioral Science (2016–2018), was awarded a Leadership in Education award by the World Education Congress in 2017, named one of the Asia Society's "Asia 21 Young Leaders" in 2018, and designated a BMW Foundation "Responsible Leader" in 2019. He delivered the commencement speech at the University of San Diego in May 2015 and TEDx Talks at TEDxAmsterdamEd and TEDxBangaloreSalon. His writing has been published in *Forbes*, the *Stanford Social Innovation Review*, MIT's *Innovations Journal*, *India Today*, and the *India Development Review*. He has been interviewed in *The Huffington Post*, *Vanity Fair*, *Forbes*, and *CNBC Africa*, among others.

Roshan has studied and worked on every continent (bar Antarctica) and is a hopeless junkie of the sport of cricket. He is the author of two books: *Such a Lot of World,* a novel, and *Your Work Begins at No,* a collection of essays on social impact education, as well as a book chapter in the anthology *Dream of a Nation: Inspiring Ideas for a Better America.*

ILAINA RABBAT

Prior to Amani Institute, Ilaina worked actively toward social change across the Americas and Europe for more than a decade, supporting individuals and organizations to increase their impact. She started her career working at the International Cooperation Department of the Youth Council of Galicia-Spain, supporting relations with the European Union. Since then, consistent with her passion for education and learning from other cultures, she has worked on community-based projects in Uruguay, Ecuador, Bolivia, and Haiti and served on the Open Society Foundation advisory board. Ilaina also worked at Ashoka as director of a youth program in Argentina, as global campaigns manager in the United States headquarters, as leader of Ashoka's expansion into Central America, and finally helped build the youth ecosystem in Kenya.

Currently, Ilaina is an advisory board member of Coca-Cola Institute (Brazil), The Bio-Leadership Project (UK), Recipes for Wellbeing (Global), the School of Future (India), and Universidad Camilo José Cela (Spain). She is a certified executive coach by the International Coaching Federation.

Ilaina has two master's degrees, one in Applied Positive Psychology from the University of Pennsylvania (United States) and one in International Studies and Peace and Conflict Resolution from Torcuato Di Tella University (Argentina). She authored a book chapter in the Brazilian anthology *Negócios de Impacto Socioambiental no Brasil*, about how social entrepreneurs can move from surviving to thriving, as well as several essays in the *Stanford Social Innovation Review*.

CPSIA information can be obtained
at www.ICGtesting.com
Printed in the USA
BVHW090229160922
646949BV00003B/19

9 781544 525174